I0014841

# Table of Contents

Copyright................................................................3

Dedication ..............................................................5

Foreword................................................................6

Introduction............................................................9

Part 1 - Threat Alert ...............................................17

The Threats ..........................................................18

Part 2 - Solutions for Individuals..........................36

Keeping It Simple ..................................................37

Easy Fixes ............................................................46

Secure Your Stored Data.......................................65

Social Media .........................................................74

Internet Browsing .................................................83

Secure Searching..................................................91

Email .....................................................................94

Secure Chat and Text...........................................112

Secure Voice Calls ...............................................119

Secure Payments .................................................125

Internet of Things.................................................132

Are You Being Held To Ransom?...........................148

CyberSafe checklist for individuals.....................158

Part 3 - Solutions for SME's..................165

SME Introduction.....................166

You are the weakest link .....................171

Secure your gates.....................177

Go phish .....................183

Get encrypted.....................188

Trading your IP for a sandwich .....................191

Don't Be Denied Service .....................198

Let's Backup A Bit.....................210

Is Your Business Being Held To Ransom?...........216

Ensure You're Insured.....................225

CyberSafe Checklist For SME's.....................229

The Last Word .....................233

Further Reading .....................235

Additional Resources .....................237

Tools And References .....................239

.....................250

Glossary .....................250

About The Author .....................301

# Copyright
## Copyrighted Material

Visit the author's website at www.expatpat.com

First Edition

Edition Date - May 2018

ISBN: 978-1722066291

Published by MOA holdings Ltd. Suite 1&2, 24th floor, 135 Bonham Strand Trade Centre, Sheung Wan, Hong Kong

Disclaimer

# Dedication

Dedicated to my beautiful wife Anthea, who supported, and encouraged me through the long nights researching and writing this book.

# Foreword

That we live in an ever more digitized world is immediately apparent if you are a citizen of Western Europe, North America or East Asia/Australasia. Accessing social media, banking, communications and retail shopping – increasingly on a smartphone – are commonplace today.

But this 'always on' scenario is not without risk. Today data is a source of wealth for many companies as valuations of the giant tech companies indicate. As in the 'real' world, criminals will take advantage whenever they see a chance to make money from stealing or denying access to data.

Nearly 2 billion files containing personal data were leaked in 2017 – and this was only in the US - and is probably under reported. Large companies and governments are addressing his issue through both technical means and training, but what can the individual citizen, owner of small and micro business do?

Pat Acheampong has the answer – plenty! An unlocked door or window is a human failure that is an invitation to criminals; similarly people are still the main cause of data theft, denial of use and therefore loss of assets and money.

Protection of your digital life is an important part of protecting yourself, your family and your assets. This clear and concise guide will go a long way to achieving that goal.

Michael Mudd

Asia Policy LLC

# Introduction

**Botnets**, hackers, **viruses**, **worms**, snoops, **trojans**, capricious governments. You've probably heard of one or all of these at one time or another. If you haven't, don't worry. By the time you've finished reading this book, you'll be well equipped to defend yourself against them, and that's what's important. They're all out there trying to invade your privacy, take over your computer, steal your identity and your cash, spy on you and map your life. This book aims to give you some tools and strategies to fight back against this online assault, and reclaim your safety online while also maintaining your right to privacy.

At a recent World Economic Forum Davos summit, a cyber security roundtable discussion revealed that the biggest banks can now expect up to two billion cyber-attacks a year; retailers, around 200 million.

Recent research from IT consultancy Cap Gemini found that only 21% of financial service organisations are highly confident they could detect a data breach.

Unfortunately, despite all the latest firewalls and antivirus software, it is we humans who are the weakest link in any organisation's security defences. Despite all the warnings, we still click on email links and attachments, download software to enable us to watch that cute kitten video, and visit websites we probably shouldn't - even while at work.

In 2013, confidential documents leaked by Edward Snowden indicated that major email and cloud storage providers like Google, Microsoft, and others were part of the NSA's top secret surveillance program called PRISM. In 2017, the U.S government passed legislation that allows internet and telecom companies to share customers' personal information, including web browsing history, without their consent. But it wasn't just governments. If that wasn't enough, there have been numerous reports of companies including well known ones such as Microsoft, and Google, snooping on their customers themselves.

All these revelations have made internet privacy a burning issue, with many privacy conscious users now turning to services that claim to be secure from prying eyes.

The first rule of internet safety, as with most other aspects of life is to keep it simple and that's exactly what this book will try to help you to do. There may be far more sophisticated ways of staying safe that the more technical amongst you are aware of, but this book is designed for the majority out there with basic technical know-how. That means that you should be able to implement most if not all of these techniques. It also means that this book is not hundreds of pages long, filled with unnecessary fluff just to pad it out. As well as keeping it simple, this book also aims to offer solutions that are practical and affordable. While there are alternative solutions available to corporations with deep pockets, this book is aimed at those without a huge cyber defence budget, either as an individual or as a small business.

These tools are a mix of **open source** and commercial applications. Woah, stop, open source? Isn't this supposed to be a guide for non-techies? Before I go any further, I suppose I should let you know what open source means. The good folks at Wikipedia have a pretty good explanation. "Generally, open source refers to a computer program in which the code used to create the program is available to the general public for use, or modification from its original design. Open source code is meant to be a collaborative effort, where programmers improve upon the source code and share the changes within the community. This code is then released under the terms of a software license. Depending on the license terms, others may then download, modify, and publish their version back to the community". Hopefully that explanation was straightforward enough without getting into more jargon. For readers with a digital version of this book, where relevant I have included the hyperlinks to tools so you can easily click on them to take you to the appropriate site.

Why use open source you may well ask, isn't commercial software better built? Well open source software can be built to just as high a standard as commercial software. Also, if the source code is available for anyone to view, it's harder, if not impossible, to hide a backdoor in the software that can allow someone to track and log your activities or even gain direct access to your computer. For example, the source code for Skype is closed so we don't really know if a backdoor is built in. With open source on the other hand, if a backdoor was built in it would quickly be discovered because of the number of coders working on it at any time.

This book is not intended to be an exhaustive list of tools you can use. There are plenty of those lists on the internet already, e.g. http://www.expatpat.com/tools. Rather, this book intends to give you, affordable, and more importantly, actionable steps you can quickly take to protect yourself and your business online.

Very few if any of the ideas and strategies in this book are my own innovations. They are pretty much proven strategies, tools, and tactics, road tested over the years by technology, security, and privacy experts. Just to be clear, simply reading this book won't make you one bit safer on the internet, or protect your data or privacy. IF, you want to achieve that, you need to take action and actually implement the strategies outlined in the book.

While every effort has been made to ensure the accuracy of the information in this book, technology evolves so fast that some services and links may be out of date. Hopefully the information you will learn in this book will give you knowledge of how to find alternatives.

## Who This Book Is For

After numerous overheard and face to face meetings with friends, family, colleagues, and clients, I came to the realisation that there are a lot of people out there that are unaware of how open they are to all the nasty stuff that can happen with your digital life, thanks to people out there with bad intentions. Or, that they knew how bad things could be, but didn't know what to do about it.

I wrote this book essentially for anyone who has concerns about their digital privacy or security. The book is aimed predominantly at individuals and small to medium business owners with little to intermediate technical knowledge and small budgets. This book will help you to effectively manage digital security in your personal life and your business.

## How To Use This Book

In an ideal world, you would have the time to read this book from cover to cover to understand the big picture around the digital threats in your online world. Obviously I recommend that you do read the whole book, but if you are strapped for time or have an urgent need to solve a specific problem I recommend the following reading plans.

- If you are just interested in protecting yourself as an individual then read parts 1 and 2

- If you are just interested in protecting yourself as an SME then read parts 1 and 3

- If you know about cyber threats and are just looking for solutions to them, then read part 2 (as an individual), or part 3 (as an SME)

# Part 1 - Threat Alert

## CHAPTER 1

# The Threats

Before we can delve into the various strategies to help keep you safe and secure online I need to give you an idea of what threats you face online. The online world is full of various terms relating to the nefarious acts of online ne'er-do-wells out to do you cyber harm. You will come across these terms on the news, while surfing, or just in conversations with friends and colleagues. Part 1 gives you an idea of what they all mean.

Viruses are harmful computer programs that can be transmitted in a number of ways. Although they differ in many ways, all are designed to spread themselves from one computer to another through the internet and cause havoc. Most commonly, they are designed to give the criminals who create them some sort of access to those infected computers.

## Spyware

The terms "spyware" and "adware" apply to several different technologies. The two important things to know about them are that:

1. They can download themselves onto your computer without your permission. This typically happens when you visit an unsafe website or via an attachment

2. They can make your computer do things you don't want it to do. That might be as simple as opening an advertisement you didn't want to see. In the worst cases, spyware can track your online movements, steal your passwords, and compromise your accounts

## Botnets

Botnets are networks of computers infected by malware (computer virus, key loggers, and other malicious software) and controlled remotely by criminals, usually for financial gain or to launch attacks on websites or networks.

If your computer is infected with botnet malware, it communicates and receives instructions about what it's supposed to do from "command and control" computers located anywhere around the globe. What your computer does depends on what the cyber-criminals are trying to accomplish.

Many botnets are designed to harvest data such as passwords, social security numbers, credit card numbers, addresses, telephone numbers, and other personal information. The data is then used for nefarious purposes such as identity theft, credit card fraud, spamming (sending junk email), website attacks, and malware distribution.

## Phishing

According to research by Verizon about 30% of phishing mails get opened. The average marketing email gets opened less than 1% of the time. How the villains behind these emails are getting this level of open rate should be the subject of a case study on marketing, but clearly they are upping their game. That's why you have this book, to help you combat this.

To summarise Wikipedia, "Phishing is the attempt to obtain sensitive information such as usernames, passwords, and credit card details (and, indirectly, money), often for malicious reasons, by disguising oneself as a trustworthy entity in an electronic communication." The word sounds like fishing due to the similarity of using bait in an attempt to catch a victim. Phishing is typically carried out by email **spoofing** or instant messaging, and it often directs users to enter personal information at a fake website, the look and feel of which are almost identical to a legitimate one. Communications purporting to be from social web sites, auction sites, banks, online payment processors or IT administrators are often used to lure victims. Phishing emails may also contain links to websites that are infected with malware.

Cyber-criminals have become quite savvy in their attempts to lure people in and get you to click on a link or open an attachment. The email they send can look just like it comes from a legitimate financial institution, e-commerce site, government agency or any other service or business. It often urges you to act quickly, because for example, your account has been compromised, your order cannot be fulfilled or some other seemingly logical reason. If you are unsure whether an email request is legitimate, try to verify it with these steps:

- Contact the company directly

- Contact the company using information provided on an account statement or on the back of a credit card

- Search for the company online – but not with information provided in the email. If it's a scam, you will often see the name come up on one of the anti-scam websites

## Spam

Spam is the electronic equivalent of junk mail. The term refers to unsolicited, bulk – and often unwanted – email.

Here are some ways to reduce spam:

- Enable filters on your email programs: Most Internet Service Providers (ISPs) and email providers offer spam filters. However, depending on the level you set in your filter, you may end up blocking emails you want. It's a good idea to occasionally check your junk folder to ensure the filters are working properly

- Report spam: Most email clients offer ways to mark an email as spam or report instances of spam. Reporting spam will also help to prevent the messages from being directly delivered to your inbox

- Own your online presence: Consider hiding your email address from online profiles and social networking sites or only allowing certain people to view your personal information. Later on in this book I discuss temporary or disposable email addresses that can be used as a potential solution to this issue

## Spam & Phishing on Social Networks

Spam, phishing and other scams aren't limited to just email. They're also prevalent on social networking sites. The same rules apply on social networks - When in doubt, throw it out. This rule applies to links in online ads, status updates, tweets, and other posts.

An increasingly popular phishing and social engineering method of scammers is the use of fake LinkedIn profiles. LinkedIn has upwards of 500 million users so is a target rich environment for those wanting to spy on companies, to those wanting to glean your personal information for identity theft purposes. In a James Bond-esque twist, the German intelligence agencies recently accused the Chinese government of trying to recruit informants on LinkedIn by luring them with fake profiles. In the chapter on social media I will cover how to try and spot LinkedIn profiles so you don't inadvertently accept a bogus connection request.

## Spear Phishing

Spear phishing is a highly specialised attack against a specific target or small group of targets to collect information or gain access to systems.

For example, a cyber-criminal may launch a spear phishing attack against a business to gain credentials to access a list of customers. From that attack, they may launch a phishing attack against the customers of the business. Since they have gained access to the network, the email they send may look even more authentic, and because the recipient is already customer of the business, the email may more easily make it through filters and the recipient may be more likely to open the email.

The cyber-criminal can use even more devious social engineering efforts such as indicating there is an important technical update or new lower pricing to lure unsuspecting victims.

## What Should You Do if You Think You are a Victim?

- Report it to the appropriate people within your organisation, including network administrators. They can be alert for any suspicious or unusual activity. Savvy companies will have set up a single point of contact so you don't have to work out who to notify

- If you believe your financial accounts may be compromised, contact your financial institution immediately and close the account(s)

- Watch for any unauthorised charges to your account(s).

- Consider reporting the attack to your local police department. These days the police tend to keep files on cyber-crime activity so they can spot trends and build up information on criminals just the way they do with offline criminals

## Social Engineering

Social Engineering is an attempt to commit fraud by obtaining information from individuals through deceptive means, such as lies, impersonation, tricks, bribes, blackmail, and threats. A social engineer will commonly use the telephone or internet to trick a person into revealing sensitive information or doing something that is against company policies and practices. By this method, social engineers exploit the natural tendency of a person to trust his or her word, rather than exploiting computer security holes.

Social engineering makes careful and thorough authentication more critical. Impersonators may:

- Claim to be from your company help desk or in a position of authority such as a senior manager

- Tell an emotional story, make you feel intimidated, or claim their computer is down and they cannot process the request or make an urgent request to encourage you to bypass appropriate verification

- Ask for exceptions to policies or procedures or try to obtain specific process information that will allow them to circumvent existing controls

- Use personal information found on social media sites to persuade team members to share sensitive information

## Chapter Summary

When dealing with cyber-crime, an ounce of prevention is truly worth a pound of cure. Cyber-crime in all its many forms just presented can at best, wreak havoc in victims' lives through major inconvenience and annoyance. At its worst, cyber-crime can lead to financial ruin and potentially threaten a victims' reputation and personal safety.

Despite our best efforts, our increasingly digital lives may put us in harm's way. The fact remains that the bad guys continue to find new uses for ever-expanding—but easily accessible—online technologies to steal, harass, and commit all sorts of crime. If cyber-crime happens to you, you need to know what to do, and to respond quickly.

Even though you may not be asked to provide evidence when you first report the cyber-crime, it is very important to keep any evidence you may have related to your complaint. Keep items in a safe location in the event you are requested to provide them for investigative or prosecutorial evidence. Evidence may include, but is not limited to:

- Cancelled cheques

- Certified or other mail receipts

- Chatroom or newsgroup text

- Credit card receipts

- Envelopes (if you received items via snail mail)

- Facsimiles (does anyone still use these??)

- Log files, if available, with date, time and time zone

- Messages from Facebook, Twitter or other social networking sites

- Money order receipts

- Pamphlets or brochures

- Phone bills

- Printed or preferably electronic copies of emails (if printed, include full email header information)

- Printed or preferably electronic copies of web pages

- Wire receipts

Once you discover that you have become a victim of cyber-crime, your response will depend, to some degree, on the type and particular circumstances of the crime. Here are some useful tips to follow depending on the circumstances of the crime:

- Make sure you change your passwords for all online accounts. You also may need to contact your bank and other financial institutions to freeze your accounts so that the offender is not able to access your finances

- Close any unauthorised or compromised credit or charge accounts. Cancel each credit and charge card. Get new cards with new account numbers. Inform the companies that someone may be using your identity, and find out if there have been any unauthorised transactions. Close accounts so that future charges are denied. You may also want to write a letter to the company so there is a record of the problem

- Think about what other personal information may be at risk. You may need to contact other agencies depending on the type of theft. For example, if a thief has access to your Social Security, National Insurance, Tax File Number etc., you should contact the relevant government department

- File a report with your local law enforcement agency. Even if your local police department doesn't have jurisdiction over the crime, you may need to provide a copy of the law enforcement report to your banks, creditors, other businesses, credit bureaus, and debt collectors

- If your personal information has been stolen through a corporate data breach (when a cyber-thief hacks into a large database of accounts to steal information, such as home addresses, and personal email addresses), you will probably be contacted by the business or agency whose data was compromised with additional instructions, as appropriate. You may also contact the organisation's IT security officer for more information

- If stolen money or identity is involved, contact a credit bureau to report the crime and request that they place a fraud alert on your credit report to prevent any further fraudulent activity from occurring. As soon as one of the bureaus issues a fraud alert, the other bureaus are automatically notified

Finally if you want to check whether your personal identity is at risk, or if you want to understand your current level of exposure to identity theft, then I suggest you use the EMC Online Identity Risk Calculator.

With all these digital threats proliferating, it's easy to think I may as well throw in the towel and go "off the grid". But there's no need to go that far. The best piece of advice I can give, is "don't be scared, be prepared". That's exactly what the following chapters are going to help you to do.

# Part 2 - Solutions for Individuals

## CHAPTER 2

# Keeping It Simple

One of the key rules in life is to keep things simple. Internet safety and privacy is no exception. So before we launch into specific tools to keep you safe, this chapter will introduce you to some simple steps you can take to maintain some level of security and privacy in an increasingly non-private world. Using these steps can help you mask your digital presence as well as keep you safe online. They don't cost much, and are fairly easy to implement even if you are not tech savvy. And yes, this does apply to you Mac users as well. Macs are not invulnerable! The internet is a powerful and useful tool, but in the same way that you shouldn't drive without buckling your seat belt, or ride a bike without a helmet, you shouldn't venture online without taking some basic precautions. Here are some simple, quick wins you can implement:

- Keep security software current: Having the latest security software, web browser and operating system is the best defense against viruses, malware and other online threats.

- When in doubt, throw it out: Links in email, tweets, posts, and online advertising are often how cyber-criminals try to compromise your personal information. Even if you know the source, if something looks suspicious, it's best to delete it or, if appropriate, mark it as junk.

- Protect all devices that connect to the internet: Along with computers, smartphones, gaming systems and other web-enabled devices also need protection from viruses and malware. See the chapter on the internet of Things (IoT) later on in this book.

- Plug & scan: USB's and other external devices can be infected by viruses and malware. Use your security software to scan them.

- When in doubt, throw it out: Links in email, tweets, posts and online advertising are often how cyber-criminals try to compromise your information. If it looks suspicious, even if you know the source, it's best to delete or, if appropriate, mark it as junk

- Think before you act: Be wary of any communication that implores you to act immediately, offers something that sounds too good to be true, or asks for personal information

- Protect your hard earned cash: When banking and shopping, check to make sure the site is security enabled. Look for web addresses with "https://," which means the site takes extra measures to help secure your information. "Http://" is not secure

- Back it up: Protect your valuable work, music, photos and other digital information by making an electronic copy and storing it safely

## Hacked Accounts

If your account has been compromised or hacked, there are various ways to regain control. But first you have to be aware that you've been hacked. So what are the tell-tale signs that your email or social network account has been hacked?

- There are posts you never made on your social network page. These posts often encourage your friends to click on a link or download an App.

- A friend, family member or colleague reports getting email from you that you never sent.

- Your information was lost via a data breach, malware infection or lost/stolen device.

If you do notice these signs and believe your account has been compromised, here are some steps you can take:

- Notify all of your contacts that they may receive spam messages that appear to come from your account. Tell your contacts they shouldn't open messages or click on any links from your account and warn them about the potential for malware

- If you believe your computer is infected, be sure your security software is up to date and scan your system for malware. You can also use other scanners and removal tools

- Change passwords to all accounts that have been compromised and other key accounts that you have ASAP. Remember, passwords should be long and strong and use a mix of upper and lowercase letters, and numbers and symbols. You should have a unique password for each account. See the chapter on passwords for advice on setting effective passwords

If you cannot access your account because a password has been changed, contact the relevant web service immediately and follow any steps they have for recovering an account.

Once you discover that you have become a victim of cyber-crime, your response will depend, to some degree, on the type and particular circumstances of the crime.  Here are some useful tips to follow depending on your circumstsncd:

- Make sure you change your passwords for all online accounts. You also may need to contact your bank and other financial institutions to freeze your accounts so that the offender is not able to access your finances

- Close any unauthorised or compromised credit or charge accounts. Cancel each credit and charge card. Get new cards with new account numbers. Inform the companies that someone may be using your identity, and find out if there have been any unauthorised transactions. Close accounts so that future charges are denied. You may also want to write a letter to the company so there is a record of the problem

- Think about what other personal information may be at risk. You may need to contact other agencies depending on the type of theft. For example, if a thief has access to your Social Security, National Insurance, Tax File Number etc., you should contact the relevant government department

- File a report with your local law enforcement agency. Even if your local police department doesn't have jurisdiction over the crime, you may need to provide a copy of their report to your banks, creditors, other businesses, credit bureaus, and debt collectors

- If your personal information has been stolen through a corporate data breach (when a cyber thief hacks into a large database of accounts to steal information, such as home addresses, and personal email addresses), you will probably be contacted by the business or agency whose data was compromised with additional instructions, as appropriate. You can also contact the organisation's IT security officer for more information

- If stolen money or identity is involved, contact a credit bureau to report the crime and request that they place a fraud alert on your credit report to prevent any further fraudulent activity from occurring. As soon as one of the bureaus issues a fraud alert, the other bureaus are automatically notified

With all these digital threats proliferating, it's easy to think "I may as well throw in the towel and go 'off the grid'". But there's no need to go that far. The best piece of advice I can give is -

don't be scared, be prepared. That's exactly what the following chapters are going to help you to do.

CHAPTER 3

# Easy Fixes

## Software updates

As much as there is reason to be leery of updates (yes, I know they can get annoying), to stay one step ahead of malicious attacks you should accept them. Every time a new security exploit comes along, operating systems (and some other programs) are upgraded to seal the hole. By not accepting these updates, you are leaving yourself open to attack.

For example the latest Windows 10 Anniversary update, has Edge exploit-mitigation features such as AppContainer sandboxing, and stronger validation built in. These have been shown by researchers to have enabled this latest Windows update to avoid falling victim to **zero-day attacks** even before the latest patches have been applied. This toolset used to be a standalone Microsoft product, but has now been built into the latest version of Windows.

All the more reason to make sure you keep your software up to date. If you're using a Mac, well you have no excuse - OS updates are free! If you need more convincing; Most of the recent victims of the recent WannaCry ransomware attack had one thing in common. They were using outdated versions of their operating system software.

## Firewalls

Your local machine needs to be guarded from local attacks. You don't have to pay big money for the "fix everything forever" **firewalls**, but you do need something. Zone Alarm makes a nice free firewall and their upgrades provide anti-virus and additional protection at a reasonable cost. Both Windows PC's and Macs also have built in firewalls. Make sure these are turned on in your settings.

If your usual firewall doesn't stop all outgoing data, get one that does. Little Snitch is an example of an excellent outgoing firewall for

Macs. Also for Mac users, Mac Keeper is a good security and privacy suite.

**For Windows PC users, take a look at Zone Alarm mentioned above.**

### Anti-virus

This is usually built into your firewall program, as it is in Zone Alarm or Mac Keeper. Now you may be thinking that you are a pretty safe web surfer so you don't need anti-virus software. I mean you never visit dodgy or risque sites. You never open emails and click on links promising you untold riches from complete strangers. Or maybe you own a Mac and have bought into the myth that Macs are immune from viruses (they're not, it's just that there are fewer Macs out there and therefore fewer virus attacks on them). But even if you are a "safe surfer" it is still a good idea to install anti-virus software, and here's why.

Even if you don't visit dodgy sites or download software of dubious origin, it is still possible for trusted sites that you visit to have been compromised. Although these days reputable companies are good at keeping up with holes in their software, there are also vulnerabilities that malevolent hackers may find (also known as zero day exploits) before they are fixed. These can be used to load malware on your computer. Remember, these days a lot of malware is created by organised crime to capture financial information and other sensitive data. Antivirus software helps you stay ahead of the bad guys by a little bit more, and is worth using.

## Passwords & Securing Your Accounts

Passwords are like keys to your home online. You should do everything you can prevent people from gaining access to your password. You can also further secure your accounts by using additional authentication methods. Passwords can be inconvenient, but they're important if you want to keep your information safe.

Better password practices shouldn't be a daunting task, so let's go through some simple ways to secure your accounts. One straightforward way is to make your password a sentence. A strong password is a sentence that is at least 12-14 characters long. Focus on positive sentences or phrases that you like to think about and are easy to remember (for example, "ComeOnYou$purs"). On many sites, you can even use spaces. Alternatively, think of a sentence or phrase that you can more easily remember. For example, "Simon really loves Italian red wine in the summertime, because he goes to Italy every year!" Then you could use that sentence as a code by inserting the first letter in each word as the password: Srllrwits,bhgtley! and then make it more secure by adding/substituting numbers and special characters for the letters. 5rllrw1t$,bhg7l3y! That's a very secure password, AND it's a LOT easier to remember. It would take centuries for a supercomputer to crack that one.

Now, obviously most people can't possibly remember dozens of cryptic passwords. That's the biggest reason why people so frequently reuse the same password over and over again across multiple websites, or even their home's Wi-Fi router. One way to remember your password is to write it down and keep it safe. Everyone can forget a password. Keep a list that's stored in a safe, secure place away from your computer. An alternative (and preferred if you're worried about your password list ending up in the wrong hands) method is to use a password manager to keep track of your passwords. Fortunately there are several password managers that exist, like 1Password, which allow you to maintain an easy, secure, encrypted database of your passwords on your own computer. The idea is that you only have to remember a single master password which allows you to decrypt the database and access the rest of your passwords. Password managers make password security much easier as long as your master password is highly secure. By the way, 1Password recently started offering a monthly subscription service to store your passwords on their servers. I recommend NOT doing this. It's much more secure to buy the software and maintain the database yourself if you can.

If you own an Apple device, then you can use Apple's keychain technology to manage your passwords. This option comes with a caveat however - If you're almost entirely using passwords only on websites, only using iOS and OS X, and don't mind memorizing and typing in passwords demanded by Apple for its services, Keychain with iCloud Keychain fits the bill. Otherwise use one of the subscription password services I mentioned earlier.

A key thing to remember is this. Unique account, unique password. Having separate passwords for every account helps to thwart cyber-criminals. At a minimum, separate your work and personal accounts and make sure that your critical accounts have the strongest passwords. The reason for this should be obvious. If you use a single password, and hackers obtain that single password, they'll be able to access your entire online life.

Once you've got your passwords sorted, there is an extra step you can take to ensure your accounts are even better protected. Lock down your login. By this I mean fortify your online accounts by enabling the strongest authentication tools available, such as biometrics, security keys or a unique one-time code through an app on your mobile device. Your usernames and passwords may not be enough to protect key accounts like email, banking, and social media. In addition, you should activate any email or SMS notifications associated with your accounts where available, so if you are hacked, you will get notified if the hacker changes any of your details.

Over time, more websites will be adopting **multi-factor authentication**. In some cases, the services may be available but are not required. Many email services also offer two-step verification on an opt-in basis. Ask your financial institution, email provider, and other online services if they offer multi-factor authentication or additional ways to verify your identity.

## Securing Your Router

I find it astonishing that despite the times we live in with all sorts of cyber criminality going on, that both individuals at home and SME's don't take one of the simplest and most effective actions in protecting themselves online - securing their wireless router. So many people either opt for a laughingly easy password to crack, or even worse, no password at all. You may be thinking, what's the worst that can happen, someone stealing my internet? Big deal, I have an unlimited data plan. Well let me enlighten you a little bit.

A hacker or scammer can drive around with a laptop computer, pick up your wireless connection from outside your home, and use it to send spam, attack servers, commit fraud, visit child pornography websites, upload or download copyrighted content, or carry out other malicious activities. These malicious activities can be traced back to your computer, and one day the police may show up at your door with a search warrant claiming that they have traced this illegal activity back to you. You may end up with a record that you were not responsible for.

Also, your neighbours may connect to your wireless internet connection to download or stream videos and movies, using up all your bandwidth. This will slow down your browsing experience and even prevent you from watching videos and anything else that requires a lot of bandwidth. If you are a business, this could seriously disrupt your business operations. Like the hackers and scammers, they can also use your wireless internet connection to commit cyber-crimes for which you may be held responsible.

## Securing Your Home Network

A protected home network means your family can use the internet safely and securely. Most households now run networks of devices linked to the internet, including computers, laptops, gaming devices, TVs, tablets, and smartphones that access wireless networks. To protect your home network and your family, you need to have the right tools in place and confidence that family members can use the internet safely and securely.

The first step is to keep a clean machine and make sure all of your internet-enabled devices have the latest operating system, web browsers and security software. This includes mobile devices that access your wireless network.

Concerned parents that also want to make sure their little darlings are not inadvertently (or deliberately!) accessing the more nefarious parts of the internet can attach internet guards to their router to monitor and control the time and content that your child accesses online. One easy to use solution that we've found is Koala Safe. It's a cost effective and easy to use - yet still effective - solution for concerned parents.

If you don't want to as far as that, and simply want to limit what your children can search for on the web, you can make sure they are using search services like KidRex or Google Junior. Both of these services sit on top of the worlds favourite search engine, but have features to limit what your children are able to search for. There are features that allow you to exclude certain keywords from searching, or for keywords that must be included in each search. To get your kids using it, just make sure it is set as their homepage on their browser.

**Secure Your Wireless Router**

A wireless network means connecting an internet access point – such as a cable or DSL modem – to a wireless router. Going wireless is a convenient way to allow multiple devices to connect to the internet from different areas of your home. However, unless you secure your router, you're vulnerable to people accessing information on your computer, using your internet service for free and potentially using your network to commit cyber-crimes.

Here are some ways to secure your wireless router:

- Change the name of your router: The default ID - called a "service set identifier" (SSID) or "extended service set identifier" (ESSID) – is assigned by the manufacturer. Change your router to a name that is unique to you and won't be easily guessed by others

- Change the pre-set password on your router: When creating a new password, make sure it is long and strong, using a mix of numbers, letters and symbols

- Review security options: When choosing your router's level of security, opt for WPA2, if available, or WPA. They are more secure than the WEP option

- Create a guest password: Some routers allow for guests to use the network via a separate password. If you have many visitors to your home, or use your home for short term rentals (e.g. AirBnB), it's a good idea to set up a guest network

- Use a firewall: Firewalls help keep hackers from using your computer to send out your personal information without your permission. While anti-virus software scans incoming email and files, a firewall is like a guard, watching for attempts to access your system and blocking communications with sources you don't permit.

## Automated forms

It sounds simple. You want to make life as easy for yourself as possible when filling in all those pesky online forms. Let's face it even though the paper forms have moved online, there are still plenty (if not more, now that it's easier and cheaper for companies to use the data) of forms that need filling. Usually these take the form of application forms for address registration, online accounts etc. Since they're online, doesn't it make sense to have a way to complete this tedious data input over and over again without having to retype everything? This is where web browser autofill comes in. Over the years browsers have been offering a way for users to store their personal data on autofill forms. The autofill system is intended to avoid tedious repetition of standard information such as your address, to be used whenever you need to complete a registration form online. Unlike traditional autofill, which just populates a single blank space in a form using previous typed-in information, an autofill profile holds much more data about you, and allows you to autofill an entire web page, often with just with one click of the button.

Hold on just a minute, before you start using these forms. Researchers have discovered recently that your browser or password manager's autofill might be inadvertently giving away your information to unscrupulous **phishers** using hidden text boxes on sites. What they have discovered is that several web browsers, including Google's Chrome, Apple's Safari, and Opera, as well as some plugins and password utilities such as LastPass, can be tricked into giving away a user's personal information through their profile-based autofill systems.

The phishing attack is actually quite simple when you think about it. Here's how it works. When you try to fill in information in some simple text boxes, such as name and email address, the autofill system will input other profile-based information into any other text boxes – even when those boxes are not visible on the page.

What this means is that when you input seemingly innocent basic information into a site, if you use the autofill systems, you could be giving away much more sensitive information at the same time. Chrome's autofill system -which is switched on by default- stores data on email addresses, phone numbers, mailing addresses, organisations, credit card information and various other bits and pieces. Do yourself a favour if you're using Chrome, and switch off this default.

At the moment, Mozilla's Firefox is immune to this problem, as it does not yet have a multi-box autofill system so it can't be tricked into filling text boxes by programmatic means. This may not always be the case however, so you should stay vigilant for future updates to see if this has changed, and update your setting accordingly.

The phishing attack still relies on users being tricked into entering at least some information into an online form, but unsuspecting users could be tricked into entering more than they bargained for relatively easily.

Fortunately this type of phishing attack has a very easy solution. Disable the autofill system in your browser or extension settings.

## Remote Wipe Your Mobile Devices

These days most people's personal and business digital lives are held on their smartphones. This makes a smartphone a particularly valuable treasure trove for identity thieves and other hackers trying to get their hands on your data for nefarious reasons. Smartphones usually come with software to remote wipe your data in the event that you lose your device and are unable to retrieve it. Even if you do retrieve it, how do you know whether the person who found it hasn't already downloaded all your data? Because of this, I recommend that you remote wipe your device as soon as you realise it's missing. If you've been following the advice in this book, you already have a backup to reload your data if you do get your device back or get a new one.

Make sure you activate any remote wiping software on your smartphone or other mobile device when you set it up. If you wait till the device gets stolen, it's too late!

If your device doesn't have software to remote wipe your data, or you are looking for an easy to use alternative that works across different operating systems and devices, I recommend installing Prey. Prey not only tracks your device and allows you to do a remote wipe, it can also help you retrieve files in the event you haven't followed the advice in this book and created a backup.

CHAPTER 4

## Secure Your Stored Data

A simple explanation of encryption is that it is the scrambling of data signals with mathematics. It is one of very few proven solutions to keep your communications private against data thieves.

There are many reasons to encrypt your files, photos, or documents. Not least to safeguard your data if you happen to lose your computer or your computer is compromised by a hacking attempt. It's not difficult to do, and I highly recommend that you do it, at least for your most important files. These days, a lot of our information is in the cloud. This makes it essential to encrypt not only the information on your computer's hard drive, but also anything you're storing in the cloud.

Another reason to encrypt your hard drive is to guard against intrusion and data theft from unscrupulous officials when traveling. This could be especially important if you have important business information on your computers which could fall in the hands of competitors through official collusion. In such instances, while full drive encryption still offers the greatest security and ease of use, it does mean that if you are ever stopped at a border with demands to see the contents of your electronics you won't be able to deny the existence of an encrypted drive.

Immigration officials in several countries - and yes this does include Australia, the USA, Canada - regularly like to poke around traveller's laptops without worrying about minor details like "probable cause", so don't assume it won't happen.

Fortunately it is possible to have the best of both worlds by setting up an encrypted container within your encrypted drive. This means you could still keep particularly sensitive data secure and invisible while being able to decrypt and hand over your laptop or hard drive for inspection.

## Encryption on your hard drive

To encrypt files containing sensitive information, you can create an encrypted file container or you can encrypt a USB drive, or your entire hard drive. On a Mac running OS X 10.7 or newer you can encrypt the whole hard drive using FileVault, Apple's built in encryption solution.

There are many solutions for encrypting your files. Below is a list of some tools for encrypting your files on your computer. This list is not intended to be exhaustive, but rather to give you some examples of effective tools that you can use today.

### AES Crypt

AES Crypt is available for desktop as well as mobile operating systems. It supports file-based encryption only, but is easy to use in that you can simply right-click files on your system to either encrypt or decrypt them.

### AxCrypt

Unlike DiskCryptor (see below), AxCrypt cannot encrypt **partitions**, only individual files. The program uses **AES 128-bit encryption** and supports key-files as well.

## BestCrypt

Unlike some of the encryption solutions presented here, BestCrypt by Jetico is not free. It supports Windows, Mac OS and Linux, and can create encrypted containers on your drive. BestCrypt also supports the creation of multiple encrypted containers which can all be mounted as virtual drives on your system.

BestCrypt also boasts additional features, including enhanced hidden containers, full version of wiping and archiving programs, and options to encrypt the Windows swap file. In addition, it also supports several algorithms including AES, CAST, Serpent, Twofish, and Blowfish. No surprise then that all this extra functionality comes at a cost. Although a commercial rather than open source product, they do publish some of their source files to provide peace of mind.

## Challenger

The Challenger program can be used to encrypt individual files, folders or drives on Windows. The project website doesn't give a great deal of information about **ciphers** and encryption algorithms used, so exercise caution if this is important to you. Challenger is free for personal use.

## CryptSetup

One in the eye this time for the more popular desktop OS's, CryptSetup is only available for Linux. It supports TrueCrypt disk formats and others. The source code is also available for those with a technical bent.

## DiskCryptor

DiskCryptor can encrypt system partitions and non-system partitions supporting all recent versions of the Windows operating system, third-party boot loaders and a lot more. For the non-techies amongst us, if you just raised your gun to your head to shoot yourself, it basically means that DiskCryptor will encrypt every part of your machine.

DiskCryptor supports several encryption algorithm and combinations, as well as hardware AES acceleration if supported by the system, and full support for external storage devices such as USB keys.

## Windows Bitlocker

Bitlocker is available in Windows Vista or 7 Ultimate, Windows Vista or 7 Enterprise, Windows 8.1 Pro, Windows 8.1 Enterprise, or Windows 10 Pro. Although there are claims that Bitlocker has a built-in backdoor for law enforcement and other agencies, these have never been proven. It does however contain recovery key functionality which can be used to decrypt drives protected by it, and which may be stored on Microsoft servers and not locally. Be aware that Bitlocker is not an open source solution if open source is a show stopper for you.

## Encryption in the cloud

If you use an online backup service, encrypt the data before you upload it. Lots of services say "we're encrypted," but that's usually only for transmission (i.e. when uploading and downloading files). Usually, your data is actually stored in a format easily readable by anyone who gets into the system (employees, hackers etc.). Given recent reports about Dropbox security, and sharing of data, be wary if you choose to store sensitive files or documents on Dropbox. Neither can Google Drive, Amazon S3, or iCloud be considered completely secure places for your data. To avoid the very worst privacy violators, you want a cloud storage provider that takes security and privacy seriously and offers strong encryption. You should also check to see whether the provider adheres to the **Zero Knowledge Standard**. Zero knowledge cloud services usually work by storing customer data in an encrypted fashion and only giving customers the keys to decrypt it, rather than the vendor having access to those keys. What this means for you is that no one, not even the company providing the storage service can get access to your data. If this is what you're looking for then check out cloud storage provider Mega. Unlike most of their competitors, their browser based encryption technology is such that you, not Mega, control the keys. Another good option to consider is Tresorit, which is Swiss-based.

Another product in this space that is worth looking at is Boxcryptor. Boxcryptor encrypts your data on your device before it is synchronised to the cloud, thereby guaranteeing the highest possible protection of your data. The software can be used with Dropbox, Google Drive, Microsoft OneDrive, and many more cloud providers. You keep full control of the content in your cloud, since it is encrypted with **AES-256** and **RSA** encryption before synchronisation. Boxcryptor also uses the zero knowledge standard.

Spideroak is a US-based cloud storage company like Boxcryptor that also offers client-side encryption. The encryption keys, as well as the password through which the keys are generated, are stored on your device, ensuring that no one, including company employees, can view your data. Spideroak supports Windows, OS X, and Linux, and has mobile apps for iOS and Android.

## CHAPTER 5

# Social Media

We live in the age of social media. There are social media sites for everything from personal, to business, and hobbies. Facebook, Twitter, Google+, YouTube, Pinterest, LinkedIn and other social networks have become an integral part of online lives. Social networks are a great way to stay connected with others, but you should be wary about how much personal information you post. The first piece of advice relating to social media is simply this. Despite the privacy claims of the most popular sites, always remember never to post anything on these sites that you want to remain absolutely private. Any information you post is available forever! This is despite the recent European Union (EU) right to be forgotten legislation. Not only that, it's available to hackers smart enough to hack the systems, governments who want access to it, and the social media platforms themselves to push advertising to you. Not to mention potential and current employers, business partners, and, yes, love interests, who may want to surreptitiously check out your background. The data you want to share with the world can be as dangerous and revealing as the data you want to keep to yourself.

For example, as an average visitor to social media websites and apps such as Facebook, LinkedIn, Twitter, Instagram, WeChat etc., chances are you share some of the following information:

- Your name
- Your date of birth
- What you look like
- Anywhere you've lived, worked, gone to school, etc.
- Your past and future travel plans
- What your lifestyle looks like
- Your interests
- Your political and religious views
- Who your friends are
- Details of family members
- Your location every time you log in. That is unless you disable location services or use a VPN. You'll read more on that later.

What more could a snoop, business competitor or identity thief ask for? So when it comes to social media, think before posting something, it can save you trouble in the future.

You and your family should follow these tips to safely enjoy social networking:

- Privacy and security settings exist for a reason: Learn about and use the privacy and security settings on social networks. They are there to help you control who sees what you post and manage your online experience in a positive way

- Once posted, always posted: Protect your reputation on social networks. What you post online stays online. Even after you've deleted it, a savvy tech person can retrieve the information. So think twice before posting pictures you wouldn't want your parents or future employers to see. Recent research found that 70% of job recruiters rejected candidates based on information they found online

- Your online reputation can be a good thing: Recent research also found that recruiters respond to a strong, positive personal brand online. So show your intelligence, thoughtfulness, and mastery of the environment

- Keep personal information personal: Be cautious about how much personal information you provide on social networking sites. The more information you post, the easier it may be for a hacker or someone else to use that information to steal your identity, access your data, or commit other crimes such as stalking

- Know and manage your friends: Social networks can be used for a variety of purposes. Some of the fun is creating a large pool of friends from many aspects of your life. That doesn't

mean all friends are created equal.
Use tools to manage the information
you share with friends in different
groups or even have multiple online
pages. If you're trying to create a
public persona as a blogger or expert,
create an open profile or a "fan" page
that encourages broad participation
and limits personal information. Use
your personal profile to keep your real
friends (the ones you know trust)
more synched up with your daily life

- Be honest if you're uncomfortable: If a
  friend posts something about you that
  makes you uncomfortable or you think
  is inappropriate, let them know.
  Likewise, stay open-minded if a friend
  approaches you because something
  you've posted makes him or her
  uncomfortable. People have different
  tolerances for how much the world
  knows about them, so respect those
  differences

- Know what action to take: If someone is harassing or threatening you, remove them from your contacts list, block them, and report them to the site administrator

- Post only about others as you would have them post about you. The Golden Rule applies online as well

Oh and here's a tip I can give that you can put into practice right now. I know going on holiday, or a business trip can be an exciting event, but NEVER post pictures of your boarding pass on social media. Not just because it tells potential criminals that you are away, but because the bar code on your boarding pass contains personal data about you that can be used by cyber-criminals who hack the code.

Earlier, in the threats section I mentioned that LinkedIn users are being increasingly targeted by fake profiles. Here are a few tips to help you spot fake LinkedIn profiles so hopefully you won't fall victim.

## A small number of connections

Scammers usually have only a single-digit numbers of connections. One of the reasons for this is that LinkedIn regularly targets fake profiles and shuts them down. If you think you've been targeted by a fake profile, help the rest of the LinkedIn community by reporting the profile to LinkedIn.

## Incomplete profile

Whole sections of bogus profiles will usually be blank. Genuine connections rarely enter information in this way. Others sections will read as if they've been copied and pasted from elsewhere, and they usually have a generic writing style with misspellings.

## Generic Job Descriptions

The job descriptions are usually written as generic job descriptions rather than a description of what the persons' role actually was or is. E.g. a sales position will describe what a salesperson does rather than the person actual sales role in the organisation

## Copy and pasted summary and experience

Often, the text used in the Summary and Experience sections are lifted verbatim, from real professionals on LinkedIn. If you are suspicious that this might be the case, copy and paste the text into google and see if a different profile comes up.

## Fake profile photos

Many fake LinkedIn accounts use unoriginal or generic profile photos. A favourite is photos of attractive young women. These profile photos are usually taken from stock image sites, other LinkedIn profiles, or other social networking sites. One way to try and verify the provenance of the photo is to use Google's Search by Image functionality.

The bottom line with LinkedIn as with all cyber-security is to be vigilant and sceptical.

If you use LinkedIn, be sceptical of who you add to your network. If you don't know the person, don't just add them. If they are a second or third degree connection, check with your other connections whether it is a valid profile or a fake one.

CHAPTER 6

# Internet Browsing

The first step to securing and anonymising your internet browsing is to choose a good browser. Browsers have varying levels of security. Keep in mind when you browse, that if the browser's lock icon is broken or carries an exclamation mark, you may be vulnerable to some adversaries that use active attacks or traffic analysis regardless of which browser you use. What's a lock icon? It's as straightforward as it sounds. A lock icon is a small picture of a padlock that appears either in the top or bottom of your browser, but usually in the search bar. If the padlock is closed, your browsing session is secure, and if it's not, it isn't. Here's a look how some of the browsers stack up.

Google and Microsoft both share their data with governments, so if that's a concern of yours it does not make much sense to use Google Chrome, Safari, or Internet Explorer.

Mozilla Firefox is a good alternative to those browsers if you're concerned about that level of privacy. It's free and open source. Another alternative is to visit the Tor Project and download the Tor Browser Bundle. The Tor browser is a version of Mozilla Firefox that has been customised to use an anonymous subnetwork which anonymises your traffic.

Here's how it works:

For example, imagine you're in Hong Kong, and you visit a website or log into Facebook via the Tor Browser. Instead of showing your IP address and location (which identifies your computer), using the Tor network might show that you are logging in from London or Sydney.

So with the Tor Browser Bundle, you do not reveal your location and identity every time you visit a website. This is very important for maintaining your privacy online.

One thing Tor cannot do though is encrypt internet traffic between the Tor network and its final destination. This means that whenever you are communicating personal information, or information you want to keep safe (for example when you log into a website with a username and password or you log into your online bank), you should make sure you are using HTTPS instead of HTTP.  What this basically means, is that you should make sure the web address starts with an HTTPS e.g. https://www.megabank.com instead of http://www.megabank.com.

One recommended plugin for the Tor Browser is HTTPS Everywhere from the **Electronic Frontier Foundation** (EFF) and the Tor Project. It also works on Firefox, Chrome, and Opera browsers. This plugin forces an https connection with many major websites and encrypts your communications.

These days, checking for secure sites is less of an issue across most browsers. Most browsers will actively warn you (or you can set preferences) when a website that does not have a security certificate (typically e-commerce sites) is asking you for secure information. However, if you want an easy, visible way to check on whether a website or link is trustworthy, consider activating Web of Trust (WOT), or CallingID on your browser.

Note to SME's - if your website doesn't have an HTTPS secure certificate, get one! You are throwing away a lot of online business if you don't. They are not particularly difficult to get, and Let's Encrypt will even allow you to get one for free.

If you are using a computer that is not your own (e.g. in an internet cafe), and you don't want to run the risk of giving away your logins when browsing the internet, a simple way to avoid being exposed is to use what are known as portable apps. A portable app is a "lite" version of a software application, which can run without being installed on the host computer. It also doesn't modify the computer's configuration information. In other words, you can run it, use it, and no-one will ever know you were there. Apart from offering more flexibility and security when working on public computers, another good use for portable apps is to keep your number of installed apps to an absolute minimum. Installed programs take up space and can cause a computer to run slower, so the less you have installed the better. There are portable apps for a number of the more popular applications. If you are using a windows PC, take a look at portableapps.com. If you are using a Mac, then you should go to freesmug.org.

## Anonymous Browsing on Mobile Devices

Browsing the web on your computer is all well and good, but these days with more and more browsing taking place on smartphones, you can still be vulnerable to unwanted intrusions. The good news is that these days, anonymous browsing is also available for smartphones.

Android

If you've got Android then you can install the Orbot and Orweb apps. Orbot lets you funnel and encrypt your smartphone traffic through the

Tor network making it anonymous, and Orweb is a web browser that's customised to work with Orbot for mobile anonymous browsing.

## iOS

If you use an iPhone or iPad (iOS) device, then check out the Onion Browser, which also enables anonymous browsing over the Tor network.

**Hiding Your Personal Online Identity Number**

If you are connected to the internet then you have an Internet Protocol (IP) address, which is the equivalent of a phone number for your computer and totally unique to you. Without it, you couldn't reach anything on the internet. Unfortunately, it's very easy for computers to grab this number and track you as you move around the internet—from the major news portals to sites of a more risqu nature.

Thankfully, there are ways to hide this using something called a **Virtual Private Network** (VPN). You may have also heard VPN services being referred to as anonymity services. These are special networks that will mask your real IP address with a fake one.

Some of these services are free; Tor (Torproject.org) and I2P (i2p2.de) are the most well-known. However, they are also difficult to use and are best left to those of a more technical bent.

There are however many cheap VPNs. The best solution is to pay for a quality system that includes the following:

• Multiple hops (bouncing your traffic between distant geographic locations)

• Out of band authentication (a special kind of login that doesn't break your anonymity)

• Your payment records and internet use records should never be in the same hands. (This is also known as no single point of failure)

One great system that fully meets these criteria is called Cryptohippie. Another option is Hotspot Shield which has a free option as well as an 'Elite' paid option. Finally there is Anonymizer. Anonymizer have been around for a long time, and have a number of options for help anonymise your browsing.

## CHAPTER 7

## Secure Searching

As you might know, Google, Yahoo, and Bing, the most popular web browsers store details about all of your searches- not only the search term itself but also your location, time and date, etc. This is done so they can "customise your search experience" and deliver targeted ads. These search engines have also been known to share data regularly with various governments.

There are however other search engines out there that you can use, that stop prying eyes from monitoring your searches. One such search engine that you should certainly consider is DuckDuckGo.

DuckDuckGo does not collect or share any personal information, and you can install their Firefox add-on in your browser. For mobile, there is also an app for iOS and Android.

Did you know that you're not only actively tracked when you search on Google or watch videos on YouTube? You are also passively tracked when you browse the web through the mass of tracking scripts that you unknowingly run, and cookies that are saved to your computer, when you visit a website. Despite EU directives that now require websites to inform you when they place cookies on your computer, how many of you really pay much attention?

Google Analytics is just one example, and it's rare to find a website today that does not have Google Analytics tracking setup. This means that you can be tracked on the majority of websites that you visit.

The best way to avoid being tracked is to block the trackers, so that you stay invisible to websites you visit. To do this, install the browser plugins like Disconnect Me or DoNotTrackMe on the Tor Browser.

One final add-on to the Tor Browser that you might want to consider is the NoScript plugin which blocks JavaScript on the websites you visit. NoScript allows **JavaScript**, **Java** and other executable content to run only from trusted domains of your choice, e.g. your home-banking web site. This guards your "trust boundaries" against **cross-site scripting attacks (XSS)**, **cross- zone DNS rebinding** / **CSRF attacks** (router hacking), and **Clickjacking** attempts

To the non-techies amongst you, what that basically means is that if you want to maximise your browser security, then you should use NoScript and **whitelist** only the websites that you trust.

## CHAPTER 8

# Email

No matter what device you use, a PC, a Mac, or a smartphone, you can get started fairly easily with encrypting your emails to prevent others from snooping on them.

First things first - if the security of your email is important to you (SME's, think commercial espionage) and you think it's a bad idea to use webmail services like Gmail, Yahoo or Hotmail (now Outlook), you're correct! Apart from being able to see the text of your email, they also record your IP address and location every time you log in to check your email. I'm sure many of you are aware (and if you weren't, you are now) of the news stories showing how Yahoo has been scanning e-mails for government checking for a while now.

Even Hushmail, a company that prides itself on offering "Free Email with Privacy", has been shown to be cooperative with governments, by handing over clear text copies of private e-mail messages at the request of law enforcement agencies. If that level of email scrutiny is concerning to you, consider closing your Google and Yahoo accounts. They are able to sell your information to anyone who pays. Instead, take your email somewhere where information on servers aren't routinely given up by your provider. Just as you can offshore your wealth to different jurisdictions to protect it, you can offshore your digital presence for the same reason. Most of the free email services people use have been implicated in government agency schemes to monitor communications. For one jurisdiction with good digital privacy laws, think Switzerland.

Hosting your email account in a jurisdiction with decent privacy laws doesn't have to be expensive or inconvenient. Some examples of reputable and relatively inexpensive options to consider such as SwissMail.org and Neomailbox.net are both based in Switzerland. Based in Norway (which also has strong privacy laws), Secure.runbox.com is generally considered a cheap and quality option.

For an email client option, you should consider using the Thunderbird email program and stop using webmail. Any mail service that you get to through your browser, rather than a dedicated mail program like Thunderbird or Outlook may have some serious security and privacy issues. Another option to consider for strong email security is Tutanota. Tutanota is an open-source alternative to Gmail that also features end-to-end "NSA-proof" encryption. However, users are limited to 1GB of online storage. Users can also send and receive encrypted attachments and can even setup their own domain server to manage business accounts. Encryption is done locally on the client end rather than through the company's server so passwords need to be strong. FastMail is an interesting alternative to Gmail—featuring a rather unique security measure to keep your messages from being data-mined. It uses YubiKey, which generates a different password (over the USB HID protocol) every time it's used, which makes it suitable for secure use with public PCs.

If you're considering the option of deleting your emails after they're sent, you might consider the following left field option. Everything you say, write, or do online is going to be discoverable long after climate change reduces this planet to a wasteland. That's why it's worth taking a look at Vanish, a tool that utterly destroys email after a short time. With Vanish you can send messages to anyone and be absolutely certain that they will evaporate from the internet within about 8 hours.

You can use the Web-based demonstration platform to get a sense of how it works. In summary, here's what happens; Type your message and click "Create Vanish Message". After a moment, you'll get a block of text that you can email to someone. They need to return to the Web site, paste the text, and decrypt it. But wait too long, and the text becomes impossible to decrypt.

If you're sufficiently intrigued, you can install the Firefox plug-in so you don't have to rely on the Web site.

Earlier in this book, I mentioned spam email and its perils. One of the ways your email address gets spammed is if companies get hold of your email address, or if companies with your email address get hacked. A solution to this is not to give out your real email address, but instead to have a disposable email address. One company that provides this service is mailinator. Mailinator provides you with a disposable email address which means that spam email should never reach your inbox. Another company in this space is ThrowAwayMail. It works by generating a disposable email address for you to send and receive email. The email address along with any emails received (so you may want to save them) will expire after 48 hours.

Encryption is all the rage right now, but encryption is only one of two steps that you need to take to secure your email. The following points will suggest some additional steps you should consider taking.

1. Move Your Email Hosting to a Secure Offshore Location

It's important to note for this point that this is only important if you have issues with government prying into your emails otherwise there is no need to go this far. Although I mention the US government, it also applies to any jurisdictions that don't have strong privacy laws. First, get your own web domain. Domain suffixes such as .no (Norway) or .at (Austria) are preferable because they are run by national-level, non-US agencies that are not under the jurisdiction of the US government.

The next step is to set up your email on an offshore server outside of your native country, and outside of the US. There are several companies that offer reasonably priced solutions for this.

One of these is NeoMailBox which has servers in Switzerland and offers secure email with built in encryption.

Another alternative is the Silent Circle. Their Silent Mail service offers state of the art encryption and comes with your own @silentmail.com email address.

However, using an offshore email provider does not guarantee privacy or security unless you encrypt your emails.

## 2. Encrypt Your Email

This is the big step. Because if you've encrypted your emails, even if someone gains access to the message, all they'll see is gibberish. Don't forget to encrypt your email drafts as well. The gold standard for email encryption is Pretty Good Privacy (PGP), or its free cousin Gnu Privacy Guard (GPG). PGP is so good that when it was first invented, the US government considered it a military-grade weapon and spent years trying to pin criminal charges on its inventor Phil Zimmerman for violating the Arms Export Control Act. Although it makes sense to encrypt your emails, it's also important to understand what is being encrypted. While secure email services boast of end-to-end encryption, the fact remains that there currently exists no way to encrypt metadata, which includes the subject line, the sender and receiver email addresses, etc.

**Encrypted Email for Desktop OS**

You can configure PGP or GPG to work with most major email clients, including Outlook, Mac Mail, and Mozilla Thunderbird.

The simplest way to get started with encrypting your emails with GnuPGP is to download and install Mozilla Thunderbird along with the Enigmail add-on, to go along with your offshore email account.

## Encrypted Email for Android

If you have a smartphone then unfortunately there are not many user friendly alternatives out there. If you are running Android there's the Open Key Chain app that works with the excellent K-9 Mail email app. They're both free, although they do require some technical proficiency to set up.

The Guardian Project also has privacy apps for Android that are pretty straightforward for everyone to use.

## Encrypted Email for iOS

If you are using an iOS device, there is iPGMail, an app that implements the **OpenPGP** standard and allows the user to create and manage both public and private PGP keys and send and receive PGP encrypted messages. iOS users also have the option of using Canary Mail (also available for Mac users) which also allows advanced users the option to create their own private keys for additional security. One of the great features of Canary Mail is that it sits on top of your existing webmail service, so you don't need to move your mail off your favourite Gmail account in order to take advantage of the security Canary Mail gives you.

## Encrypted Email in the cloud

Of course not everyone wants to use email on their desktop, and increasingly cloud email services are the go to solution for most people. Does this mean you are then restricted to Outlook (formerly Hotmail), Gmail, or Yahoo!? Bearing in mind that Yahoo has already admitted to over a billion of their email addresses being hacked, this may well give you pause. The good news is that no you are not restricted to these providers for cloud email, and there are secure cloud based email providers that you can use.

Protonmail is one such example. Protonmail is open-source, and provides end-to-end encryption, that allows users to encrypt messages in their web browser before the information reaches the company's servers in Switzerland. It also has free mobile apps, so you're not tied to your desktop if you want to use their secure services.

When you send an encrypted message to somebody who is not on Protonmail, they receive a link that loads the encrypted message onto their browser, which they can decrypt using a decryption password that you have previously shared with them. Of course, you can also send unencrypted messages to Gmail, Yahoo, Outlook, and others, just like regular webmail.

As a final word on selecting an email service, here are some key points to keep in mind when selecting one:

- Free is unrealistic. If a service is "free", be wary

- Freemium can only be supported by paying customers, meaning that paying customers also have to support all the freemium customers

- You may be forced to use email only with a browser, not with the standard native applications on your desktop, phone, or tablet that you're already using and are familiar with

- The location of servers in a "secure datacentre" in a country with "strong privacy laws" may be helpful but isn't a guarantee. The only true data protection is an encryption key known only to you

## Avoiding Email Scams

I'm sure you're all familiar with the email scams that are sent from all over the internet by scammers trying to trap the unwary into clicking on them. They range from trying to get you to email them sensitive private information, to installing malware on your computer to allow your computer to be remotely controlled or your private information stolen. There are three main types of scams for you to look out for.

1. Email asking you for personal or financial information

In this example you generally get an email from someone in distress that needs your help; or someone in a corrupt country who needs to transfer a large sum of money out through a third party bank account - i.e. yours!; or a letter telling you that you have received a large sum of money, usually an inheritance or lottery win or some form of compensation payment. These messages usually end with a request for you to contact them for further information or to provide your bank details so they can deposit the money in your account. Sounds simple right? Well so is the solution. If it's not already in your junk folder, then consign it there, where it belongs.

2. Official looking email from an institution you belong to or use (e.g. a bank)

Usually this takes the form of an institution or service that you use sending you a message. Often they require you to click on a link to verify your ID or to reset your password etc. There are two possible ways to check the authenticity of these types of mail. The first is to hover over any link they send you without clicking on it. If you're using a decent email service, the url for the link should show up on the bottom of your email window. That way you'll be able to easily see that the url is redirected to the scammers url. The second way is to simply call the relevant institution to verify if they have sent an email.

There are some tell-tale signs to look out for that are typical characteristics of scam emails:

- If you have not heard the name of the company before, search on Yahoo, Google or Bing to see if the company has a genuine website. Also check if other people have reported that the company has been involved in scams previously. Websites like snopes are great for checking on scams

- The mail asks for your personal, non-work related information such as credit card numbers or bank information over phone or email

- If the mailer has used free email IDs to either contact you or as 'reply to' email IDs. For example, if you get a job offer from XYZ Petroleum Company, and their email ID is xyzpetroleum@gmail.com or xyzpetroleum@yahoo.com then it is most probably a fake company. Real companies use their own domain name on their email, and do not use free email providers

- If the 'reply to' email ID is different from the 'from' email ID

- If the contact telephone numbers are mobile phone numbers

- If the mailer asks for money-transfers, or payment for any unsolicited service upfront, such as immigration and visa processing, travel, model portfolio pictures etc.

- If the mail offers jobs without a face to face interview

- If the mail offers things you have not applied for

- If the mail offers unrealistic amounts of remuneration, benefits, gifts etc.

3. Email from a friend asking you click on a link

This one can sometimes be the hardest one to spot. You get a seemingly innocuous email from a friend or contact asking you to click on a link in their email. This usually happens when their email account has been hacked and emails are sent to their address list. Should you click on the link? The first thing to think about in this case is how well do you know your friend? Is this the sort of email they would send? If not, ignore the email. If you're not sure, simply drop them a message (preferably using an alternative service to the one that just got hacked) to see if they're aware of the email.

Remember, if in doubt throw it out, and follow these simple pieces of advice:

- Don't reveal personal or financial information in an email, and do not respond to email solicitations for this information. This includes following links sent in email

- Before sending sensitive information over the internet, check the security of the website. Does it have the locked padlock icon on it?

- Pay attention to the website's URL. Malicious websites may look identical to a legitimate site, but the URL may use a variation in spelling or a different domain (e.g., .com versus .net)

- If you are unsure whether an email request is legitimate, try to verify it by contacting the company directly. Contact the company using information provided on an account statement, not information provided in an email. Information about known phishing attacks is also available online from groups such as the Anti-Phishing Working Group.

## CHAPTER 9

# Secure Chat and Text

I can see what you're thinking. Forget about email, if I want to send something confidential to my business partners or friends, I'll just use instant messaging (IM). Believe it or not, even your IM, and text messages are not secure from snooping. Because of that, you'll need to learn how to securely chat, call and text whether you're using your laptop, Android, or iOS device.

If you are currently using Facebook chat, Skype, Google Talk, MSN, or regular texting to chat with your friends, then your conversations can be read like open book.

A previous version of this book mentioned Whatsapp in the list of chat apps that can be read like an open book. The good news is that Whatsapp have recently upgraded their app to include end-to-end encryption of your messages. If you haven't upgraded to the latest version yet, I suggest you do.

## Encrypted Text

If you are texting between Android smartphones then take a look at TextSecure by Whisper Systems. TextSecure is a free and open source app by Open Whisper Systems. It will not only encrypt your text messages locally on your phone, but also encrypt them over the air, for full privacy. So if you lose your phone, your text messages will still be protected with full encryption, as long as you choose a good password!

However, even though your text messages will be encrypted, your phone company and other snoops, hackers, and ne'er-do-wells will still be able to see that it was you who sent the message. They will also be able to see who received it so you can still be profiled, even though they don't know what you're talking about.

If that's an issue for you, use one of the following instant messaging solutions instead. All these solutions use what is known as **Off-**

the-Record (OTR) cryptographic protocol, and when combined with Tor, no one will be able to know who you are, who you are talking to, or what you're talking about.

The best thing is, with any of the solutions mentioned (except for Cryptocat), the OTR protocol is platform independent, which means you can chat on your iPhone with someone using an Android, PC, or Mac, as long as they also have a client that supports OTR.

### Encrypted Chat for Desktop OS

If you want a really easy solution that just works, then use Cryptocat. It's an easy to use IM client that encrypts your communication with the OTR protocol mentioned earlier (non-techie alert: if you don't know what this is, you don't need to worry about it!), and like many of the other recommendations in this book, it's free and open source.

To get started you can either install the Firefox plugin for your Tor Browser or if you have a Mac you can download the Cryptocat application in the app store.

It's important to know though, that this is not a perfect solution. As the website points out -

"Cryptocat does not anonymize you: While your communications are encrypted, your identity can still be traced since Cryptocat does not mask your IP address. For anonymization, we highly recommend using Tor.

Cryptocat does not protect against keyloggers: Your messages are encrypted as they go through the wire, but that doesn't mean that your keyboard is necessarily safe. Cryptocat does not protect against hardware or software keyloggers which might be snooping on your keyboard strokes and sending them to an undesired third party.

Cryptocat does not protect against untrustworthy people: Parties you're conversing with may still leak your messages without your knowledge. Cryptocat aims to make sure that only the parties you're talking to get your messages, but that doesn't mean these parties are necessarily trustworthy."

According to the EFF -

"The easiest way to use OTR encryption [on a laptop] is to use Pidgin or Adium for your IMs (Pidgin is a program that will talk to your friends over the MSN, Yahoo!, Google, Jabber, and AIM networks; Adium X is a similar program specifically for Mac OS X)."

If you're using Pidgin, install the OTR encryption plugin for that client. Adium comes with OTR built in.

Once OTR encryption has been installed, to ensure proper network privacy you will need to make sure the people you are talking to also use OTR encryption. From then on, it's pretty straightforward. Simply follow the OTR encryption instructions to "Confirm" any person you need to have sensitive conversations with. This reduces the risk of an interloper being able to trick you into talking to them instead of the person you meant to talk to. For example you can do this just by agreeing on a shared "secret squirrel" word that you both have to type.

Jitsi is also a good open-source alternative with OTR support, that can also be used for encrypted voice and video calls.

## Encrypted Chat for Android

If you have an Android smartphone and want to chat in private, then the ChatSecure app is what you're looking for. ChatSecure can be used regardless of whether you use Facebook Chat, Google Chat, Hyves, Jabber, VKontakte, Yandex, Odnoklassniki, StudiVZ, Livejournal, WeChat etc.

## Encrypted Chat for iOS

Similar to Android, the ChatSecure app for iPhone and iPad is an open-source app that uses the OTR protocol for encrypted instant messaging.

## CHAPTER 10

# Secure Voice Calls

This chapter is only going to deal with VoIP calls, i.e. calls made over the internet, because even if you encrypt calls over the regular mobile phone network your telecom provider stores who you talk with, when you talk, and your physical location. Also, the scope of this book as mentioned earlier is online privacy and security.

As mentioned previously, if absolute security is important to you, don't use the big commercial services like Skype or Google Voice.

Why? Well the main reason is because despite the fact that they do encrypt your voice calls there are still open questions on their rumoured backdoor ability to grant requestors the privilege of listening in on your calls. If this is not an issue for you, then Skype's encryption will protect you from hackers not granted permission by Skype. Another service that has just joined the big boys is Whatsapp. You know they're secure, when even governments try to stop them operating because their service is too secure.

If you don't want to use any of the big commercial services, then there are other more secure alternatives, many of them using the Open Secure Telephony Network (OSTN) and the server provided by the Guardian Project. If you're interested in that level of security simply go to their site and follow the straightforward instructions to get yourself set up with the service.

## Encrypted Voice Calls for Desktop OS

To encrypt your voice calls on your desktop, one recommendation is to use the open source Jitsi app which can encrypt your voice and video calls over OSTN. Once you have done that, sign-up with a VoIP provider like Diamondcard.us that accepts anonymous payments to allow you to pay for the service. Of course if you're only looking for secure calls, not anonymity, you can ignore the diamond card option.

## Encrypted Voice Calls for Android

If you are using Android, there are a couple of recommendations for you to use to encrypt your calls. One is the CSipSimple app for Android which enables you to communicate securely over OSTN. You can download the app from the Google Play store.

An alternative solution for Android is the free RedPhone app by Open Whisper Systems. It's also open source. One note of caution though. RedPhone only encrypts the traffic between your phone and the other end of the line. As the Tactical Technology Collective puts it:

"It becomes easier to analyse the traffic it produces and trace it back to you, through your mobile number. RedPhone uses a central server, which is a point of centralisation and by doing so, it puts RedPhone in a powerful position (of having control over some of this data)."

## Encrypted Voice Calls for iOS

For encrypted iOS calls, you will need to look at a different solution to those mentioned above. The Groundwire app for iPhone and iPad will allow you to receive encrypted voice calls over OSTN. An additional in-app purchase will unlock the ZRTP extension that will allow you to also place secure calls.

## Platform Independent Voice Call Encryption

Not all voice call encryption tools are limited to a specific platform. This is especially useful as an SME if you have a mix of platforms within your business. If platform independence is important to you, then the solution you may want to look at is Silent Phone. Silent Phone is part of the Silent Circle and they have apps for both iOS, and Android.

119

The app works over 3G, 4G, or WiFi networks. As part of the Silent Circle suite you will also find Silent Eyes for Windows that enables encrypted video chat(Mac users, see Jitsi mentioned previously), and Silent Text (currently only for iOS) .

Another offering in this space - Wire, is backed by the guy who was responsible for co-founding Skype - Janus Friis. Envisioned as a modern-day take on Skype (had it been built today) the upgrade to Wire will allow users on Chrome, Firefox, and Opera web browsers to both make and receive calls, while IE and Safari users are only be able to chat at this time.

In addition to making calls and chatting, Wire users on the web will be able to create and leave group conversations, as well as block users. Also, like mobile apps, Wire offers push notifications where supported.

Wire was designed with the goal of creating a communications platform that leverages newer technologies than those used by older services like Skype, which is now more than a decade old. Following that approach, most of the new features are under-the-hood improvements in areas like media compression, audio technology, file delivery and more. It is backed by a team whose backgrounds include time spent at Apple, Skype, Nokia and Microsoft, so you would expect them to know what they're doing.

There are also a couple of other noteworthy applications in this space that are worth mentioning. These services are Hushed and Guardlock. While both are secure and will stop your personal or business calls being snooped on, they are also relatively new services so we will see if they stand the test of time.

## CHAPTER 11

## Secure Payments

If you're worried about your online payments being hijacked or tracked, then the straightforward solution to this is...whenever possible, pay in cash. By not using your credit card for every purchase, you remove yet another source of data that can be tracked and stored indefinitely.

So what's the alternative? Well one alternative to consider is paying in **Bitcoin**, if possible.

Bitcoin is a digital currency that is completely decentralised. There is no Bitcoin issuer that regulates its supply like a central bank, and no shadowy elite that has the power to conjure new Bitcoin out of thin air.

The full details on working with, and learning about Bitcoin are beyond the scope of this book. To get started on using Bitcoin, and to learn a little more about it in depth, visit the bitcoin.org website.

If however you are familiar with the workings of Bitcoin, you may still be wary due to all the stories that have begun to emerge about bitcoin being hacked and people losing all their money. If that is your thinking, then the main thing you need to bear in mind is that Bitcoin itself was not hacked. Rather, it was the exchanges that held the Bitcoins that were hacked. That being the case, what you need to do is to protect yourself against your private crypto key being stolen or hacked, and your Bitcoin being stolen from your e-wallet.

One of the simplest and most effective ways to secure your private key is to ensure that your private key is stored offline, and not kept on a web service or online wallet. This is known as cold storage. With this option, you go to a site like Warp Wallet, or Bit Address and take the following steps:

- Load the page and disconnect your computer from the Internet. This ensures no one online can spy on your activity

- Once the site has gone through the process to generate a key, you should select the option which chooses a paper wallet

- Print your paper wallet, and put it in a safe place

Now that your paper wallet is secure, your Bitcoin is offline and safe from Cyber criminals. If you don't feel up to going through these steps, then the best I can advise you is to store your Bitcoin across several exchanges or mobile wallets. That way if one gets hacked; at least you won't lose everything.

## Online Shopping

As previously pointed out in this book, it's important to take steps to protect yourself when shopping online.

Anything connected to the internet, including mobile devices like smartphones, and tablets need to be protected – especially during heavy use periods like the festivals and holidays. Scammers and cyber-criminals can and do target shoppers as well. Everyone should be on alert for emails that might get us to act quickly and click through links and open attachments as mentioned in the chapter on email. Be wary of emails about problems with your credit cards or an account or the status of online order. The bad guys know we are price sensitive when shopping online, so exercise caution when you see an advertised offer where the discount is way below normal. Basically, what I'm saying is take reasonable security precautions, and think about the consequences of your actions online so you can enjoy the conveniences of technology with peace of mind while you shop online. Remember these tips during all online purchases:

- Conduct research: When using a new website for purchases, read reviews and see if other consumers have had a positive or negative experience with the site

- When in doubt, throw it out: Links in emails, posts and texts are often the ways cyber-criminals try to steal your information or infect your devices

- Personal information is like money, value it and protect it: When making a purchase online, be alert to the kinds of information being collected to complete the transaction. Make sure you think it is necessary for the vendor to request that information. Remember, you only need to fill out required fields at checkout

- Use safe payment options: Credit cards are generally the safest option because they allow buyers to seek a credit from the issuer if the product isn't delivered or isn't what was ordered

- Don't be disappointed: Read return and other polices so you know what to expect if the purchase doesn't go as planned

- Protect your hard earned cash: When shopping, check to be sure the site is security enabled. Look for web addresses with https:// indicating extra measures to help secure your information. If the site url does not begin with https:// when you're required to put in sensitive personal or financial information, DON'T USE IT.

## Shopping On the Go

- Now you see me, now you don't: Some stores and other locations look for devices with Wi-Fi or Bluetooth turned on to track your movements while you are within range. Disable Wi-Fi and Bluetooth if you don't need to use it

- Get savvy about Wi-Fi hotspots: Limit the type of business you conduct over open public Wi-Fi connections, including logging on to key accounts, such as email and banking. Adjust the security settings on your device to limit who can access your phone

CHAPTER 12

# Internet of Things
## What Is The Internet of Things

<u>The Internet of Things</u>(IoT) has been an industry buzzword for years. If you own a smartphone, a laptop, a printer, and a smart TV, you already live in a smart home. The rise of the IoT will bring with it huge benefits to businesses and consumers, but right now it is also creating a security nightmare. As sensors and connectivity have become cheaper, it has become more viable to add them to a far wider range of devices than ever before. So the 'things' in the IoT can range from consumer goods like baby monitors, thermostats, and cars through to industrial systems.

There are plenty of good reasons to connect such devices to the internet. For example, a connected thermostat allows you to warm up the house before you get home, while a factory could reduce downtime if sensors warn that a critical machine is about to overheat.

New "things" being deployed everywhere are exploding the range of areas that can be attacked. Gartner forecasted that 6.4 billion connected things will be in use worldwide in 2016, growing to 20.8 billion by 2020. In 2016, 5.5 million new things will get connected every day. The IoT is creating a tremendous digital business future where interactions between things we wear, touch or utilise become integrated into the digital business fabric. As IoT grows, security risks grow with it.

## The IoT Threat

You have a video baby monitor, and a wireless security camera too? All these connected devices are your IoT and they all need protection. The horror stories have already started.

The baby monitors transmitting a live feed onto the internet for all to see; the smart teddy bear that could be hijacked; the car that allows hackers to take control of systems remotely; the power grid knocked offline by attackers accessing industrial control systems. 70% of IoT devices are open to attacks and Global IoT Security spend is expected to reach $840 million by 2020 according to Gartner report.

Parents have always worried about their children choking on a small part of a toy, but there are new dangers to worry about with the next generation of toys. Many kids' toys today are smart toys connected to the home's network, through which a hacker can gain entry into the family's home.

Once in control of a toy, a hacker will have access to smart TVs, mobile phones, computers, tablets, gaming systems — literally everything that is connected to the home network. And these devices aren't always safe. In fact, many of them leverage the cloud for security. The device's security is also tied to, and reliant on, the security of the manufacturer's use of cloud and Software as a Service (SaaS) offerings.

For those thinking this is a far-off scenario, it's not. There are examples of recent IoT breaches, such as compromised dolls, or the VTech data breach that exposed the personal data of 12 million people, including 6.4 million minors. In each of these cases, the privacy of children has been called into question.

A grey-hat hacker going by the name of Stackoverflowin, **pwned** over 150,000 printers that had been left accessible online. Luckily for the owners of the printers, his intentions weren't malicious; he just wanted to raise everyone's awareness towards the dangers of leaving printers exposed online without a firewall or other security settings enabled. For 24 hours, he ran an automated script which searched for open printer ports and sent a rogue print job to the device. This hack affected high-end multi-functional printers at corporate headquarters to lowly receipt printers in small town restaurants.

Researchers have already demonstrated that smart meters widely used in Spain, for example, can be hacked to under-report energy use. They were able to spoof messages being sent from the meter to the utility company and send false data. In recent years we have been able to go to a high street store and buy anti-virus protection on a disc or download it straight to our PC. But in the IoT that security capability doesn't exist in many of the devices that will suddenly become connected.

Another great and detailed example was the hack of a car wash carried out by Billy Rios of Laconicly car wash. The kind of car wash with huge brushes, foam and so on. Today's car washes have smart control systems which are connected and, consequently, susceptible to a remote hack. If successful, a hacker obtains full control over all aspects of the car wash's operations. There are vast opportunities to do whatever they want, including getting services free of charge, as the owner account has access to various tools, including a payment system. They can hold a car being washed inside the car wash, after obtaining control over the gates. There's even the possibility of breaking the car wash or damaging a car, as a car wash facility is equipped with a number of moving components and powerful engines.

Is there anything else to hack? Sure, anything you want! For instance, at the Security Analyst Summit 2015, Vasilis Hiuorios, a security expert at **Kaspersky** Lab reported his hack of a police surveillance system. The police hoped that beam antennas were enough to secure communications.

If the police are so careless as to allow hacks of their networks and appliances, it goes without saying that gadget makers are even more so. Another Kaspersky's expert, Roman Unuchek, demonstrated a hack of a fitness band at SAS 2015: after a series of relatively simple tricks one can connect to a fitness band and download information about the owner's location tracking.

In general, the problem is that those who develop home appliances and make them connected face realities of a brand new world they know nothing about. They ultimately find themselves in a situation similar to that of an experienced basketball player sitting through a chess match with a real grand master.

Things get even worse when it comes to the users of connected devices. They don't bother with security at all. For an average user, a connected microwave is still just a microwave. A user would never imagine it is a fully-equipped connected computer which has means of influencing the physical world.

There are a flood of appliances which are connected without a thought whether it's necessary or not.

The problem has become so serious that the US Federal Trade Commission has kicked off a competition to create tools that consumers can add to their home network that can protect IoT devices from attack. Cash rewards of $25,000 (£20,000) will be given to the best entrants.

"There isn't any category of devices that has not been hacked to some degree: we're talking anything from lightbulbs to nuclear power stations. As soon as you connect something to the internet then it's hackable and it's a target" says Duncan Brown, research director at analyst firm IDC.

Or, as Jeff Jarmoc, a Salesforce security engineer, tweeted, "In a relatively short time we've taken a system built to resist destruction by nuclear weapons and made it vulnerable to toasters." That's funny, but it's no joke.

Many good security tools and techniques are available in the market today to protect you from IoT hacks, but the new threats can't be conquered with old tools and techniques. Your new security opponent will be a smart machine, so your new defender must be an algorithm. Security firms have launched routers that can stop smart household gadgets being hijacked by hackers.

## Data collection, protection and privacy

The vision for the IoT is to make our everyday lives easier and boost the efficiency and productivity of businesses and employees. The data collected will help us make smarter decisions. But this will also have an impact on privacy expectations. If data collected by connected devices is compromised it will undermine trust in the IoT. We are already seeing consumers place higher expectations on businesses and governments to safeguard their personal information.

Your fitness watch is monitoring and storing critical health data including your heart rate, activities and performance with every second of its use. You can't even imagine the amount of data that might be getting generated every moment by all of your IoT devices combined.

Also, the company that collects data may choose to abuse the data, or sell the data to someone with a foul intent. Another possibility could be, a company that collects the data for legitimate reasons may get hacked, and the hacker steals the stored data.

Connecting IoT devices also introduces new risks. For consumers there is a risk to privacy as these devices will record vast amounts of data about their daily lives that could be pieced together to create a deeply intimate portrait of their existence. For businesses, each of these new devices is a potential gateway into your network for hackers to exploit, and potentially allow them access to not just data but also the controls to physical systems where they could do real damage.

## IoT Security Solutions

Sooner or later, the impact of all these unsecured connected systems could be detrimental. Most people barely give a second thought that a hack of a smart-connected appliance could be dangerous and a lot more threatening than a simple PC hack.

For users, some of the best advice is limiting the use of way too 'smart' connected tech. That may not be practical for a majority of users though. If you fall into the latter group, then you will have to buy a security solution for your internet-of-things.

To help IoT users deal with the threat, Symantec, BitDefender, and Intel have unveiled devices that scrutinise data as it flows across home networks. The companies say routers with built-in defences will be essential as homes are filled with net-connected gadgets. The routers also come with parental control features that help manage how much time children spend online and what they access.

As the entry and exit point for home networks, routers are the best place to put a security system that can watch for malicious traffic coming in and cut off hackers trying to access insecure IoT kit. While current home routers do have security systems, most are pretty basic, and virtually none are ready for the explosion of smart devices predicted to be in use soon.

Bit Defenders' solution to protecting your IoT products is their Box tool. The theory is that just by plugging in the Box to your network, you have the protection of an entire antivirus suite, at a lower cost, and without the effort of installing software on every device. Its Private Line feature offers the protection of a VPN, with the assurance of your own trusted network. And it claims to solve the problem of having dozens of internet connected devices that can't be secured through traditional means. As far as I'm aware, it's the first device of its kind, and I hope it won't be the last.

Box's Private Line feature extends malware protection to your Mac, Windows, and iOS devices that are currently out of range of your protected Wi-Fi network, for example when you leave home and access a different network. Once enabled, your traffic is routed through and protected by the Box no matter where the device is or how it's connected to the internet (be it Wi-Fi or cellular). It's your very own VPN service.

What BitDefender is targeting is devices that can't protect themselves, but still contain valuable personal data. Bitdefender claims that the Box protects every device, including your printer, your desktop computer, your laptop, your sundry smartphones, your various tablets, your gaming consoles, your Nest smart thermostat, your smart fridge, your Philips Hue lights, and so on. Many of these devices are completely closed to the user and can't have antivirus protection installed.

If something untoward happens to any of the connected devices, Bitdefender will block the threat and send you a message through the app.


## A Final Word on IoT

The threat level is not the same for all devices and there are countless considerations to take into account; would someone rather hack your daughter's teddy bear, or something a bit more serious? It's necessary to reduce data risk, keep as much personal data as possible from IoT devices, properly secure necessary data transfers, and so on.

Kaspersky has been sounding alarm bells for a while, backing them up with examples of hacked smart homes, carwashes and even police surveillance systems. Whether a hacker wants to wash their ride free of charge, or stalk someone using their fitness tracker – IoT security flaws could make it possible.

Besides the solutions mentioned earlier, here are some additional things that you can do to secure your IoT devices:

- Where possible, lock down IoT applications and operating systems. Just like any server, the device should have the absolute minimum of network services. Your smart TV may need to use DNS, but your smart baby monitor? Not so much

- Check your device documentation. If it allows you to change the default password, make sure you do. See the earlier chapter on passwords

- Make sure that the contact information for all of your devices are up-to-date including an email address regularly used to receive security updates and related notifications

- Confirm all your devices and their mobile applications are set for automatic updating to help maximise protection. Review their sites for the latest firmware patches. If they are not automatically updated, follow the instructions to manually update them

- Review the privacy policies and practices of your devices, including data collection and data sharing with third parties. Your settings can be inadvertently changed during updates. Reset as appropriate to reflect your preferences

- Review devices' warranty and support policies. If they are no longer supported with patches and updates, disable the device's connectivity or stop using the device

- Before discarding, returning or selling any device, remove any personal data and reset it to factory settings. Disable the associated online account and delete any associated data

143

- Review privacy settings on your mobile devices including location tracking, cookies, contact sharing, Bluetooth, microphone, and other settings. Set all your device and applications to prompt you before turning on and sharing and data

## CHAPTER 13

# Are You Being Held To Ransom?

If you've been paying attention, you would've noticed the steady stream of news around hacking and cyber security. And if you're one more step engaged, you'll notice a hot buzzword that incites great fear into those who know it's a lurking threat (cue dramatic music) - **ransomware**.

Ransomware is one of the biggest problems on the web right now. It's a form of malicious software -- malware -- which encrypts documents on a PC or even across a network. Victims can often only regain access to their encrypted files and PCs by paying a ransom to the criminals behind it.

In a ransomware attack, the hackers gain access to the victim's computer and encrypt its files. The hackers then charge the victim to decrypt the files, which only they can do.

Throughout 2016, ransomware attacks made news by forcing money out of private and public organizations, including a hospital in Los Angeles and the public transportation system in San Francisco. Once they've infected a system, hackers typically demand payment via anonymous bitcoin.

A report by SonicWall, a cyber security firm report identified 638.2 million unique ransomware attempts in 2016, up from 3.8 million in 2015.

In a 2016 report on ransomware and businesses, Symantec commented that "The past 12 months have seen ransomware reach a new level of maturity and menace". Can you hear the screams? Yikes.

As I was doing research on ransomware, I was surprised to learn that you and I - the consumer - are a more likely victim of ransomware than companies, accounting for 57% of all infections between January 2015 and April 2016. I had assumed that businesses were the more likely target.

That's not all. The virality of the malware and the size of the ransom keeps going up exponentially, year after year. The average ransom in 2016 stands at nearly USD$700, this is more than double the amount from about USD$300 in 2015. Even then, there is no guarantee you will get your files back after you pay.

I don't know about you but I don't want to pay a hacker almost USD$700 for files or photos that I am not even guaranteed to get back, when there is an easy, affordable action that only 20% of people take. What is that action? It's simple - regularly backing up your files both online in the cloud and offline locally (see the chapter on secure backups for more information). If you are infected with ransomware or crypto malware, it doesn't matter. You don't have to even consider paying because you have everything on your computer securely backed up, and up-to-date. High-five! Feels good, doesn't it?

As I mentioned earlier in this book, don't be scared of ransomware, just be prepared.

Whether you're looking for ransomware prevention, protection, or defence, or you want to avoid a hard drive failure or another catastrophic data loss scenario, backing up your data is one of the smartest decisions you will ever make. Take 15 minutes today to protect your most important files, folders, photos, movies, music, you name it.

Home users and small businesses using Windows should run Windows Update, ensure their antivirus software is up to date runs a scan, and to also consider backing up data. The exploit code used by **WannaCrypt** is designed to work only against unpatched Windows 7 and Windows Server 2008, or even earlier systems such as Windows XP.

The FBI put out a Public Service Announcement (alert number I-091516-PSA) on ransomware in September 2016, listing ways you can defend yourself or your business.

West Coast cyber risk modelling firm Cyence estimated the average individual ransom cost from Friday's attacks at $300, and the total economic costs from interruption to business at

USD$4 billion.  That's got to be worth it to put your mind at ease surely.

## What is a ransomware attack?

A ransomware infection often starts with you or someone with access to your device (desktop or mobile) clicking on what looks like an innocent attachment. But that's not the only way to get infected.

## A brief history of ransomware

While ransomware exploded in 2016, increasing by an estimated 750 percent, it's not a new phenomenon; the first instance of what we now know as ransomware appeared in 1989.

Known as AIDS or the PC Cyborg Trojan, the virus was sent to victims -- mostly in the healthcare industry -- on a floppy disc. The ransomware counted the number of times the PC was booted: once it hit 90, it encrypted the machine and the files on it and demanded the user 'renew their license' with 'PC Cyborg Corporation' by sending USD$189 or USD$378 to a post office box in Panama.

In the biggest ransomware attack to date, WannaCry - also known as WannaCrypt - also known as WannaCry and Wcry - caused chaos across the globe in an attack which started on Friday 12th May 2017.

Wannacrypt ransomware demands USD$300 in Bitcoin for unlocking encrypted files - a price which doubles after three days. Users are also threatened, via a ransom note on the screen, with having all their files permanently deleted if the ransom isn't paid within a week.

More than 300,000 victims in over 150 countries fell victim to the ransomware on over the course of one weekend, with businesses, governments, and individuals across the globe all affected. Healthcare organisations across the UK had systems knocked offline by the ransomware attack, forcing patient appointments to be cancelled and hospitals to tell people to avoid visiting Accident &

Emergency departments unless it was entirely necessary.

Of all the countries hit by the attack, it was Russia which was hit the hardest according to security researchers, with the WannaCry malware crashing Russian banks, telephone operators and even IT systems supporting transport infrastructure. China was also hit hard by the attack, with an estimated 29,000 organisations falling victim to this particularly vicious form of ransomware.

What all the targets had in common is that they were running unsupported versions of Microsoft Windows, including Windows XP, Windows 8 and Windows Server 2003.

## Bitcoin and ransomware

The rise of crypto-currencies like Bitcoin has made it easy for cyber-criminals to secretly receive payments extorted with this type of malware, without the risk of the authorities being able to identify the perpetrators. The secure, untraceable method of making payments - victims are asked to make a payment to a bitcoin address - makes it the perfect currency for criminals who want their financial activities to remain hidden.

## Getting rid of ransomware

The No More Ransom (NMR) initiative launched in July 2016 by Europol and the Dutch National Police in collaboration with a number of cyber security companies including Kaspersky Lab and McAfee, offers free decryption tools for ransomware variants to help victims retrieve their encrypted data.

NMR initially launched as a portal offering decryption tools for four families of ransomware - Shade, Rannoh, Rakhn, and CoinVault. The scheme regularly adds more decryption tools for even more versions of ransomware including Crypt XXX, MarsJoke, Teslacrypt, Wildfire, and Nemucod.

The portal, which also contains information and advice on avoiding falling victim to ransomware in the first place, is updated as often as possible in an effort to ensure tools are available to fight the latest forms of ransomware. NMR has grown from offering a set of four tools to carrying 54 decryption tools covering 104 families of ransomware. So far, these tools have decrypted more than 28,000 devices, depriving criminals of over GBP£7m in ransom. The platform is now available in over 26 languages with more than 100 partners across the public and private sectors supporting the scheme.

Individual security companies also regularly release decryption tools to counter the ongoing evolution of ransomware - many of these will post updates about these tools on their company blogs as soon as they've cracked the code. For example, another decryption tool recently released may be able to help if your PC has been hit by one of the original versions of the Petya malware (the so-called Red Petya, Green Petya, and GoldenEye) and may enable you to recover your lost files. However, these tools don't always work, so another way of working around a ransomware infection is to ensure you regularly back up your data offline.

## Can you get ransomware on your smartphone?

Desktop computers are not the only way to pick up ransomware; your mobile devices are also susceptible. Ransomware attacks against Android devices have increased massively, as cyber-criminals realise that many people aren't aware that smartphones can be attacked and the contents (often more personal than the stuff we keep on PCs) encrypted for ransom. In fact, any internet-connected device is a potential target for ransomware, which has already been seen locking smart TVs. For more information on that, see the previous chapter on the Internet of Things

# CyberSafe checklist for individuals

The checklist below summarises the content from the individual section and shows you where to find it. You don't need to action on all of it, but clearly the more you complete, the more secure you will be.

| Action | Chapter Ref | Done |
|---|---|---|
| Install/ turn on your firewall | 3 | |
| Download your latest OS patches | 3 | |
| Install an antivirus or update your | 3 | |

| Action | Chapter Ref | Done |
|---|---|---|
| antivirus to the latest definitions | | |
| Change your passwords to strong passwords | 3 | |
| Select and use a password manager | 3 | |
| Enable multi factor authentication on all available services | 3 | |
| Add a secure password to your home router | 3 | |

| Action | Chapter Ref | Done |
|---|---|---|
| Set up a guest network on your home router | 3 | |
| Disable form autofill in your web browser | 3 | |
| Encrypt your hard drive | 4 | |
| Backup your data securely in the cloud | 4 | |
| Backup your data securely locally | 4 | |
| Switch to a more | 6 | |

| Action | Chapter Ref | Done |
|---|---|---|
| secure internet browser on your computer | | |
| Switch to a more secure browser on your mobile device | 6 | |
| Install a VPN | 6 | |
| Switch to an online search service that doesn't track you | 6 | |
| Switch to a secure email service or client | 8 | |
| Switch to secure | 9 | |

| Action | Chapter Ref | Done |
|---|---|---|
| chat on your device | | |
| Switch to secure voice calls on your device | 10 | |
| Change default passwords on your IoT devices | 12 | |
| Update Firmware on your IoT devices and set them to automatically update | 12 | |
| Stop using IoT | 12 | |

| Action | Chapter Ref | Done |
|---|---|---|
| devices not covered by a warranty | | |
| Set mobile device and application settings to prompt you before sharing data | 12 | |
| Check your identity risk score | 1 | |

# Part 3 - Solutions for SME's

## CHAPTER 14

# SME Introduction

In 2016 McAfee labs counted an average of 400,000 distinct new incoming cyber threats per day; a decade before, it was 25 per day. A billion personal records are now stolen each year, degrading trust in the organisations victimised and the internet itself. The scope of cyber-attacks has broadened exponentially, too. Where once individual retailers or banks were targeted, now entire supply chains, financial networks, and stock markets may be in the crosshairs, potentially affecting the integrity of international financial systems or a country's GDP.

If you're a small business owner, and you're thinking this will never happen to you, here are some statistics that might give you pause, and convince you to take action to protect your business:

- Attacks on businesses go undetected for an average of 144 days

- Compromised business emails are up over 1300%

- Over 90% of analysed phishing emails in Q1 2016 contained ransomware

- Around 40% of small businesses were targeted by hackers

- 1 in 8 enterprises suffered a security breach due to a social-media related cyber attack

If there's one thing that you should keep in mind when thinking about internet threats, it's this; assume that you WILL get attacked at some time. With that in mind, you need to be crystal clear on governance - who is responsible for your businesses cyber security? You need to ensure you have a very clear policy on escalation and when to call in external entities, e.g. law enforcement; lawyers; PR; I.T security firms etc.

Many businesses neglect this, but if you use third party vendors for your critical systems or supply chain, then you need to assess the risk factors associated with these vendors. This may be challenging to do, but even a rudimentary audit should catch the most glaring issues. If a supplier is unwilling to provide this information, then it is worth your while to re-think whether you want to be in that business relationship.

The rise of the mobile workforce has made it challenging for I.T teams to protect data that is created outside of the business's firewall. Simplifying data protection for laptops and mobile devices begins with providing backup to your mobile workforce, and giving I.T one place to manage all of their device's data protection needs.

An increasing area of threat for SME's is the Internet of Things (IoT). As IoT devices are always connected and always on, they go through a one-time authentication process making them perfect sources of infiltration into organisation's network. Therefore, these gateways need to be better secured in order to improve the security of the overall system.

There are software such as WhiteOps which monitor the network data flow, identify malicious bots, flag suspicious files, and analyse them for destructive or malicious intentions; invest in them. These may seem like small measures, but they play a big role in the overall IoT security strategy.

If all else fails, at least be prepared for potential security breaches. Sooner or later they will happen, to you or someone else (well, preferably a competitor). Always have an exit strategy, a way of securing as much data as possible and rendering compromised data useless without wrecking your IoT infrastructure. You should also educate customers, employees, and everyone else involved in the process about the risks of such breaches. Instruct them what to do in case of a breach, and what to do to avoid one. Employees (in particular any employee that touches data), should take a cyber-awareness course to increase their awareness of the risks, and to improve the cyber security of your business.

Of course, a good disclaimer and Terms of Service (TOS) will also help if you end up dealing with the worst-case scenario. For more information on IoT and how you can protect yourself, see the chapter on IoT earlier in this book.

Those are the basics. The following short chapters give you some more detailed advice on how to protect your business that any developing company or established SME and its leadership team could and should adopt.

## CHAPTER 15

# You are the weakest link

Yes you...well to be fair, you and your employees, not just you. You can have all the best technology in place, but until artificial intelligence takes over running the planet, this technology relies on humans to be a little bit smart about how they use it to minimise risks. Unfortunately too many companies neglect this education in favour of crossing their fingers and hoping that nothing bad happens.

## Workplace Security Risk Calculator

If you'd like to find out how much you or your employees are unwittingly putting your company at risk, then I suggest you take a look at the EMC Workplace Security Risk Calculator. Another extremely useful resource to gauge your businesses cyber security readiness is the Small Business Internet Security Planner. This resource will walk you through step by step; the various aspects of cyber planning you can use to protect your business.

## Employee Collaboration

Some small businesses like to use social media as a way to engage both employees and customers. This makes sense since most people use social media these days. But, there are alternatives to using commercial social media networks, and you can find software that allows you to create walled off social media networks without spending a fortune. An example of this is Dolphin by Boonex. Depending on your level of technical skill and your appetite for security, they have both an on premise version, and a cloud version. Bitrix24 offers a similar solution, or for something open source, take a look at exo Platform.

## Employee Browsing Info

Get information about your employees' browsing activity. This allows you to see information about how long users are browsing, and on which sites they spend their time. Even if you don't use this sort of information to "spy" on your employees, it can help locate potential sources of an attack on your systems by tracing which sites were accessed.

## Data Loss Prevention

These types of services from companies such as Mcafee, Symantec, End Point Protector, and Digital Hands allow you to set the rules about, and vet everything that your employees put on the web. This helps prevent unauthorised company information being inadvertently or deliberately posted in the public domain.

Lost or stolen mobile devices are the most common source of reported data leaks. This could take the form of anything from employees leaving their mobile on a bus, to a laptop being stolen from a bar or coffee shop. With the proliferation of mobile devices, this makes safeguarding data a potential nightmare for any SME without a large I.T. department to help them manage these devices. Smartphones usually come with software to remote wipe data in the event a device is lost, but that is more often than not on an individual basis. As a business, you want to be able to manage this on a business wide level not only if a device is lost, but also if an employee leaves your business. This is especially important in the age of Bring Your Own Device (BYOD) where employees keep business and personal data on the same device.

One previously recommended service that can be used for managing your digital assets is Prey. Prey not only tracks your device and allows you to do a remote wipe; it can also help you retrieve files in the event you haven't followed the advice in this book and created a backup. Another service I recommend for SME's is the Absolute platform product Computrace. A great feature of Computrace is that it is BIOS level software. This means that even if a thief were to reformat the laptops drive and reload windows, the BIOS will see that Computrace is not loaded into windows anymore and will reinstall it in the background so you can still trace your device and wipe the data.

## Get An Education

I can't stress enough the need to get yourself and your employees educated on cyber security. It should be one of the first things you do when on boarding a new employee. In fact I would go so far as to suggest that no new employee should be let loose on your systems until they go through your cyber security education course.

If you're thinking that these courses will be too much for your already stretched budgets, I would hope that the information you've read in this book so far and the information in the following chapters will convince you of the cost of not having staff that are adequately trained and aware of the cyber threat every business faces these days. Besides, not all cyber security courses require the brains of Einstein or the budget of IBM. In fact some of the courses are even free. To show how seriously I take this, I've done some of your homework for you. Here are some courses to consider:

The British government provides free training courses:
https://www.gov.uk/government/collections/cyber-security-training-for-business

If government provided training isn't your thing, Future learn also provide a free online course with optional paid upgrades:
https://www.futurelearn.com/courses/cyber-security-business

These are just two examples of cyber security training for SME's. As you can see, they don't have to cost an arm and a leg. So do yourself a favour and get yourself an education. After all, what is your business worth to you?

## CHAPTER 16

# Secure your gates

There are barbarians at the gate. It stands to reason, that if you are going to spend a lot of time, money, and effort to secure the various parts of your infrastructure that you don't just hand the keys to the front door to the "cyber-barbarians". To help ensure that this doesn't happen, you need to spend time securing logins that people use to enter your systems in the first place. We've already covered how humans are the weakest link, well this chapter should help you and your employees learn how to keep your systems secure. Here are some useful strategies to use.

## Implement access management

No matter how lean or open a work environment you strive to create, not everyone needs to be an admin for everything. The most sensible security rule recommended to startups is to thoughtfully assign services, and then individual logins, instead of sharing the same username and password across an entire company. If you're serious about security, then stop sharing usernames and passwords today. Seriously, stop. That 10 dollars a month for an extra user will seem like the world's biggest bargain if you get hacked and your business is held to ransom.

Why go through the hassle of extra logins? Well, because all companies - no matter how generous your compensation and benefits, or innovative your technology - experience turnover. As a business owner, having to be forced to scramble to change access for all personnel each time an individual departs, particularly in the case of a disgruntled employee - or soon to be ex-employee - who has access to your proprietary and critical IT, IP, and other key data is not something you or your business can afford to waste time on. What's even worse is if you decide it's too much effort, and leave your business wide open to I.T misuse. When properly applied, access management allows startups and SME's to tailor permission levels. Most of the collaboration tools listed in http://www.expatpat.com/tools allow you to do this. Two examples of good ones to look at are Bitrix24, and Exo Platform. If however, you're using multiple tools already and need to secure them all, then using a tool like One login will help you get control of your company's login security.

## Enforce two-factor authentication

Two factor authentication (2FA) does exactly what it sounds like - it requires a user to provide a second level of authentication when logging on to their businesses systems in addition to a username and password - This typically takes the form of a token with a numerical code, a smart card, a text message to a phone or even a biometric (think thumbprint or iris) scan.

2FA is especially for critical systems like email, databases, cloud providers, and social media accounts. Requiring a password and a device - what you know and what you have - can halt a ne'er do well before they can break in, and let you know something is wrong early on. Imagine being able to thwart the damage caused by credential theft from a phishing attack or malware - that's the beauty of 2FA. If you're looking for a recommendation for 2FA, take a look at ID Key. It's a biometric password manager with a range of features to help secure your systems.

## Use a password manager

As previously mentioned in the chapter on passwords for individuals - it's the 21st century. No two passwords should be the same, and there's no reason to have a password with fewer than 12-14 characters including letters, numbers, and special characters, or one that references your favourite child, your pet, that celebrity you fancy, or any word in the Oxford English Dictionary.

One straightforward way for your employees to create strong passwords is to make the password a sentence. A strong password is a sentence that is at least 12-14 characters long. Focus on positive sentences or phrases that you like to think about and are easy to remember (for example, "ComeOnYou$purs").

Alternatively, think of a sentence or phrase that can be more easily remembered. For example, "Simon really loves Italian red wine in the summertime, because he goes to Italy every year!" Then you could use that sentence as a code by inserting the first letter in each word as the password: Srllrwits,bhgtley! and then make it more secure by adding/substituting numbers and special characters for the letters. 5rllrw1t$,bhg7l3y! That's a very secure password, AND it's a LOT easier to remember. It would take centuries for a supercomputer to crack that one. So in addition to 2FA, insert a password management system like 1 Password or Encryptr by Spideroak into your company's security policy.

Password managers are software services that generate and securely store long, complex passwords in an encrypted virtual container. Its beauty is that your employees need to remember only one - hopefully robust - password to unlock the manager. They can then cut-and-paste or auto-fill into the individual sites and services that they use. Password managers solve the problem of complex passwords. For peace of mind in your business, make sure everyone in the company is using one.

## CHAPTER 17

# Go phish

No not the kind where you use a rod and line, although Phishing attacks do involve a digital hook, line, and sinker. For a quick primer on what Phishing is, see the phishing section in chapter 1 at the beginning of this book.

According to the Microsoft Computing Safer Index Report 2014, the annual worldwide impact of phishing could be as high as $5 billion. With numbers like that, you want to make sure that your business is not one of those that falls victim to a Phishing attack. So what can you do to reduce the chances of this happening?

The weakest link in a Phishing attack is people - that means your employees. The first line of defence is to educate them on phishing attacks and how to avoid them. Here are some of the things you can train your employees to look out for:

- Spelling and bad grammar - Cyber-criminals are not known for their grammar and spelling. Professional organisations usually have a staff of copy editors that will not allow a mass email like this to go out to its users. If you notice mistakes in an email, it might be a scam

- Beware of links in email - If you see a link in a suspicious email message, don't click on it. Rest your mouse (but don't click) on the link to see if the address matches the link that was typed in the message. If the addresses don't match, there's a good chance it's a scam. Links might also lead you to .exe files(.dmg files for Mac users). These kinds of file are known to spread malware

- Threats - Have you ever received a threat that your account would be closed if you didn't respond to an email message, or that you owe money to the government and you need to click on a link to fill out a form? Cyber-criminals often use threats that your security has been compromised in order to panic you into clicking on a compromised link

- Spoofing popular websites or companies - Scam artists use graphics in email that appear to be connected to legitimate websites but actually take you to phony scam sites or legitimate-looking pop-up windows. Cyber-criminals also use web addresses that resemble the names of well-known companies but are slightly altered to try to fool you into clicking on them

People being people however, means that despite training your staff in what to look out for, you are going to need a second line of defence, and that means software to help you avoid phishing attacks. A lot of large organisations have large cyber defence teams that run fake phishing attacks on their employees to find vulnerabilities, as well as having heavy duty software to mitigate attacks. As an SME, what you need is software that is easy to use, and also relatively inexpensive.

One recommended software suite to consider is inky. One of the good things about inky, is that it is designed to work with your existing email system. It also works cross platform, so whether your business uses Windows, macOS, iPhones, or Android phones, it will work for you.

Aside from technology solutions, here's a simple solution that even the most technophobe amongst you can get behind. Use the phone. Train employees to call whenever a request for sensitive data or materials, like wire transfers, passwords, or personal data, are requested by another party. It doesn't matter if the request is coming from the email address of someone you share a cubicle wall with; email can be hacked (unless you've been implementing the strategies I've shown you earlier). When someone actually does need access to a service - e.g., they need your 2FA code to get into Twitter - and they send a note to you asking for those credentials, call and speak to them.

Especially at a small startup, where you know everyone's voice, verbal confirmation is the most effective way to avoid getting phished by someone using **social engineering** tactics.

## CHAPTER 18

# Get encrypted

## Using encryption for sharing sensitive information

GPG Tools as mentioned earlier work really well for protecting your information, and you should be using encryption for more than just your emails. Even if your company communications are happening behind 2FA, and you use logins with complex, unique passwords, bad things can still happen. If you're sharing any sensitive information, encrypt it, because if another party is phishing you, they get nothing without the intended recipient's private key. And if the communications service provider (e.g. email, Slack, Yammer etc.) gets hacked, you don't have to worry about your critical keys being stolen.

Using a software suite like paubox, will go some way to helping you relieve your encryption headaches. Because their solution covers HIPAA

184

compliant email, forms and storage, it means that you don't need to go to individual providers for all those services.

## Using full-disk encryption

Mobile phones get lost. People leave laptops alone on coffee shop tables. Tablets are stuffed into airplane seat pockets and forgotten. Stuff happens. And when stuff does happen, whether it's a minor irritation or major disaster for your company depends on how well you've prepared. These machines hold your company's intellectual property, strategic plans, and access to email, keys, and communications, essentially the lifeblood of your company.

Likewise, make sure your devices require passwords to turn on and wake from sleep. Make sure that all your staff are aware that they should lock their machines every time they step away from them. Yes you trust the guy sitting next to you, but if you're away from your desk and so are they, who's to stop someone else coming in and doing what they shouldn't?

I'd encourage you to encrypt backups too. This comes as a built-in feature on modern operating systems and on backup drives (like Apples Airport Time Capsule, and Western Digital external drives), so someone can't pick up your external hard drive and wander off, or make a copy while you're away from your desk.

As mentioned earlier in this book in the chapter on encryption, modern operating systems, such as macOS, Windows 10, iOS and Android, come with full disk encryption. Use it, and make sure everyone in your company is using it - it's free!

## CHAPTER 19

# Trading your IP for a sandwich

Startups and the more progressive companies, with their flex-time and work-from-wherever attitudes are great at giving employees the freedom to do their jobs from wherever they want. Hey, why not, since there's free Wi-Fi on practically every corner. But, as anyone who's ever tried to get something for nothing will tell you, there's never any such thing as a free lunch.

Take for example Firesheep. No, not a dodgy anti-Ovine group from the green, green pastures of Wales. Firesheep is a free program that lets hackers grab cookies from non-encrypted code, and gain access to your private information. That means anyone in proximity to an employee on public Wi-Fi can potentially access that individual's (i.e. you) - or even your company's - Facebook, Twitter, and LinkedIn accounts.

Worse still, hackers can create rogue-yet-legit-looking Wi-Fi hotspots ( i.e. beware anything called "Free Public Wi-Fi") so when you connect to the company network while munching down your bacon and egg sandwich with a flat white, they can see any data you share and receive over this connection. There are some straightforward solutions to this:

- Ensure that you and your employees always use a VPN when connecting to external Wi-Fi. With an anonymous browsing service, websites won't be able to figure out your IP address or location. They will only be able to see information about the servers belonging to the VPN company that you use, instead of your company's servers

- Do not connect to anything called "Free Public Wi-Fi"

- If your data plan supports it, tether to your phone as a hotspot

Even better, invest in a solution like Privacy-as-a-Service platform Dispel. Dispel encrypts both data and connections for all employee daily browsing, email, file transfers, messaging, and social media, segmenting and isolating each device from neighbouring users.

And here's a bonus tip. Not to be Captain Obvious, but please train your employees not to click sketchy links, or download weird things from the internet. And do revisit the earlier chapter on anti-virus software, and follow the recommendations.

This one should almost go without saying, but it's really important so I'll put it here anyway. The internet is full of nasty stuff, and people with bad intentions. Practicing good digital and device hygiene is essential for keeping your data safe. Train all your employees to cultivate a healthy amount of scepticism when downloading software. Better yet, either track or remove the ability for unauthorised staff to download unauthorised software. Keep an eye out to make sure website SSL certificates are valid, and don't forget to install a high quality anti-virus scanner, even Mac users. Why? Because you never know.

## CHAPTER 20

# Safe Commerce

## Secure Certificates

As mentioned earlier in this book, if your website doesn't have an HTTPS secure certificate, get one! Especially if you have a transactional website and you are expecting customers to input sensitive credit card and personal information. You are throwing away a lot of online business if you don't. They are not particularly difficult to get, and Let's Encrypt will even allow you to get one for free.

## Escrow Payments

An additional level of security that you can apply to your B2B transactions is to use escrow payments. As defined in investopedia, Escrow is a legal concept in which a financial instrument or an asset (in this case you money) is held by a third party on behalf of two other parties that are in the process of completing a transaction. The funds are held by the escrow agent until it receives the appropriate instructions or until predetermined contractual obligations have been fulfilled. Money, securities, funds, and other assets can all be held in escrow.

When parties are in the process of completing a transaction, there may come a time when it is only of interest for one party to move forward if it knows with absolute certainty that the other party will be able to fulfil its obligations. This is where the use of escrow comes into play.

For example, a company selling goods internationally wants to be certain that it will get paid when the goods reach their destination. Conversely, the buyer wants to pay for the goods only if they arrive in good condition. The buyer can place the funds in escrow with an agent and give irrevocable instructions to disburse them to the seller once the goods arrive. This way, both parties are safe, and the transaction can proceed.

Now this may seem like a rather cumbersome way of managing your payments, but especially with more and more business being international these days even for SME's it could be a good protection for your company especially if you are not sitting on large cash reserves to turn to if a transaction goes bad. Thankfully there are payment companies that will help you easily manage escrow payments. Two good services that are worth looking at if you choose to turn to an escrow service provider are the services provided by escrow.com and payoneer.

## CHAPTER 21

# Don't Be Denied Service

Cyber security experts knew major destructive attacks on the internet were coming. The first of them hit Dyn, a top-tier a major Domain Name System (DNS) service provider, with a global **Distributed Denial of Service (DDoS)** attack.

As Dyn went down, popular websites such as AirBnB, GitHub, Reddit, Spotify, and Twitter followed it down. Welcome to the end of the internet as we've known it.

Like mobile phone service and tap water, most of us have assumed that the internet was as reliable as our electrical power. Although depending on which country you're reading this in, that may not be a good analogy. Those days are over. Today, we can expect massive swathes of the internet to be brought down by new DDoS attacks at any time.

But knowing the basics of a DDoS, and being equipped to deal with a large scale attack of this type are two very different things. While large sites are often attacked, it's important that those businesses and networks do everything they can to deflect them and remain accessible, even under heavy loads. For you managing a smaller (but still critically important) site, as a small business, you never know when cyber criminals will decide to go after you. Fortunately, you can do some things about it, so let's take a look at some of the important details behind what a DDoS truly is, and some methods that can be used to make sure your business network is safe from them.

## Defending your intranet and websites

First, you should protect your company site(s) by practicing DDoS prevention 101. For example, make sure your routers drop junk packets. You should also block unnecessary external protocols such as Internet Control Message Protocol (ICMP) at your network's edge. And, as always, set up good firewalls and server rules. In short, block everything you can at your network edge.

Better still, have your Internet Service Provider (ISP) block unnecessary and undesired traffic. For example, your ISP can make your life easier simply by **upstream blackholing**. And if you know your company will never need to receive **UDP traffic**, like Network Time Protocol (NTP) or DNS, your ISP should just toss garbage traffic into the bit bin.

If this is all too techie for you, you should look to DDoS mitigation companies to protect your web presence. Companies such as Akamai, CloudFlare, and Incapsula offer affordable DDoS mitigation plans for businesses of all sizes.

Amazon's answer is the AWS Shield service. AWS Shield will protect your cloud instances from DDoS attackers. Unlike the other services mentioned above, AWS Shield is only for AWS customers. At the time of writing, all AWS customers receive AWS Shield Standard automatic protections free of charge; so your cloud instances should be safe from most such attacks.

What Amazon brings to the DDoS battle-line is the sheer scale of Amazon Web Services (AWS). This family of services makes up the world's largest public cloud.

That's fine for protecting your home turf, but what about when your DNS provider gets attacked?

As DDoS attacks grow to previously unseen sizes, even the DDoS prevention companies are being overwhelmed. Akamai, for example, had to stop trying to protect the Krebs on Security blog after it was smacked by a DDoS blast that reached 620 Gbps in size.

Another way to mitigate these attacks is by using multiple DNS providers. One way to do this is to use Netflix's open-source program Denominator to support managed, mirrored DNS records. This currently works across AWS Route53, RackSpace CloudDNS, DynECT, and UltraDNS, but it's not hard to add your own or other DNS providers. This way, even when a DDoS knocks out a single DNS provider, you can still keep your sites up and running.

There are also companies out there that provide redundant DNS that you can use. Check if your DNS provider does this. Which options will work best for you? You can find out by using Namebench. This is an easy-to-use, open-source DNS benchmark utility.

One simple way you can try to keep these DNS attacks from being quite so damaging is to increase the Time to Live (TTL) in your own DNS servers and caches. Typically, today's local DNS servers have a TTL of 600 seconds, or 5 minutes. If you increased the TTL to say 21,600 seconds, or six hours, by editing your DNS settings, your local systems might dodge the DNS attack until it was over.

As a business, you should really consider a DNS provider that is not your Domain Registrar or your Hosting Company. Also, you should have your Zone Files mirrored at your hosting company just in case the DNS provider goes down. You can quickly update the DNS record to point to them while the DNS provider issues are resolved.

## Web-based Malware Prevention

The value of malware prevention tools or services is in protecting your network from **drive-by downloads**, Java and Flash exploits, and any other threat on the web. According to Wikipedia, drive by downloads generally fall into two main categories:

1. Downloads which a person authorised but without understanding the consequences. E.g. downloads which install an unknown or counterfeit executable program, **ActiveX** component, or Java applet automatically.

2. Any download that happens without a person's knowledge, often a computer virus, **spyware**, malware, or **crimeware**.

Drive-by downloads may happen when visiting a website, viewing an e-mail message or by clicking on a deceptive pop-up window in the mistaken belief that, for example, an error report from the computer's operating system itself is being acknowledged or a seemingly innocuous advertisement pop-up is being dismissed. In such cases, the "supplier" may claim that the user "consented" to the download, although the user was in fact unaware of having started an unwanted or malicious software download. Similarly if a person is visiting a site with malicious content, the person may fall victim to a drive-by download attack. That is, the malicious content may be able to exploit vulnerabilities in the browser or plugins to run malicious code without the user's knowledge.

## Virtualisation

Businesses trying to ward off millions of dangerous cyber-attacks in an increasingly connected world have struggled to find a solution to isolate all the malicious websites and emails that their employees access every day. Perhaps now, they do have one.

A cyber security firm called Bromium reckons its technology can protect laptop and desktop users against malware hidden in email attachments and compromised websites.

It does this through a process called **micro-virtualisation**. Every time you open a document or visit a website, Bromium creates a mini protected virtual environment for each task. What this means is that even if you've clicked on an email link containing a virus, there's nowhere for that malware to go because it is isolated within its virtual bubble. It cannot infect the rest of the machine or penetrate the corporate network.

If you'd like to find out how secure your website is, and how to improve its security, UpGuard have created a website risk grader that you can use to gauge your websites vulnerability to risks. The tool is free to use for individual company scans.

## Protecting the internet

While these techniques might help you, they don't do that much to protect the internet at large. To gain even greater protection, check whether your ISP and router and switch vendors have implemented Network Ingress Filtering, better known as Best Current Practice (BCP)-38.

BCP-38 works by filtering out bogus internet addresses at the edge of the internet. So, when your compromised webcam starts trying to spam the net, BCP-38 blocks these packets at your router or at your ISP's router or switch. To check if your ISP has already implemented BCP-38, try running Spoofer. This is a new, open-source program that checks to see how your ISP handles spoofed packets. BCP-38 isn't a cure-all, but it does help.

Another fundamental fix that could be made is response rate limiting (RRL). This is a new DNS enhancement that can shrink attacks by 60 percent. RRL works by recognizing that when hundreds of packets per second arrive with very similar source addresses asking for similar or identical information, chances are they're an attack. When RRL spots malicious traffic, it slows down the rate the DNS replies to the bogus requests; Simple and effective.

## How to protect your network

So as you can see, a DDoS can take multiple forms, and when building a defence against them, it's important to consider these variants. The easiest -albeit costly- way to defend yourself, is to buy more bandwidth. A denial of service is a game of capacity. If you have 10,000 systems sending 1 Mbps your way that means you're getting 10 Gb of data hitting your server every second. That's a lot of traffic. In this case, you want more servers, spread around various data centres, and you want to use good load balancing. Having that traffic spread out to multiple servers will help the load, and hopefully your bandwidth will be large enough to handle all that traffic.

Finally, you should also think about ways to mitigate any attack that does reach your site. For example, most modern websites use a lot of dynamic resources. While the actual bandwidth from an attack may be manageable, often what ends up failing is the database, or the custom scripts you may be running. Think about using caching servers to provide as much static content as possible. Have a plan in place to quickly replace dynamic resources with static ones, in the event that you're getting attacked. And make sure to have detection systems in place. The worst thing for any business is for the network or site to go down, so you want to be alerted as soon as an attack starts, and be ready to deal with it.

Because of the way it's done, halting a DDoS attack at the source is incredibly difficult. But setting up an infrastructure that is distributed, hardened, and secure is possible, and that's something you should think about when setting up your network.

Those are some basic ideas on how to mitigate DDoS attacks on your business. It's now up to you to use them. Don't delay. Bigger attacks are on their way and there's no time to waste.

## CHAPTER 22

# Let's Backup A Bit

The subject of securing your stored data is discussed in the chapter on securing your stored data. But let's summarise some of it for SME's. One of the smartest things you can do as a business is to protect yourself against data loss by making electronic copies of important files, commonly referred to as a backup.

Our computers contain vast amounts of data, from family photos and music collections to financial records and personal contacts. In fact, a recent National Cyber Security Alliance/Symantec study found that more than 68% of Americans store 25% or more of their photos digitally. For most people, the loss of that information could be devastating. For an SME, it could be the complete loss of your business.

Data can be lost in several ways: computer malfunctions, theft, viruses, spyware, accidental deletion, and natural disasters.

Data backup is a simple, three step process:

1. Make copies of your data

2. Select the hardware or method to store your data

3. Safely store the backup device that holds your copied files

Let's go into these in a bit more detail.

## Make Copies of Your Data

Many computers come with a backup software program installed, so check to see if you have one. Other software programs are available for purchase if your system does not have a backup program or if you're seeking other features. Ideally, you should backup your files at least daily.

Most backup software programs will allow you to make copies of every file and program on your computer, or just the files you've changed since your last backup.

## Select Hardware to Store Your Data

When you conduct a backup, the files will have to be stored on a physical device - such as CDs, DVDs, or USB flash drives, an external hard drive, or on the web using cloud-based online storage.

- CDs, DVDs and flash drives: These are best for storing a small amount of pictures, music, and videos

- External hard drive: It's a good idea to get an external hard drive to back up all your critical business files. This way, you can assure more adequate secure storage for all your files. Copying information will also be faster with these devices

- Online backup services: If you don't want the hassle of new hardware, there are many online backup services available, usually for a monthly fee. Some security software includes this service with your subscription, so be sure to check that you don't already have this service available. You simply backup your files to a secure server over the internet. These services have the added advantage of safely storing your files in a remote location and the files can be accessed anywhere you have a connection to the internet. This can be valuable if you or your employees travel a lot and may need to recover files or if your business is in area prone to natural disasters that might require an evacuation.

**Safely Store the Backup Device that Holds Your Data**

After setting up the software and copying your files on a regular basis, make sure you keep your backup device somewhere safe and secure, preferably off your business premises. Keep your backup device close enough so that you can retrieve it easily when you need to retrieve your data.

For some companies, putting all these strategies together -straightforward though they are - as individual solutions can seem overwhelming. Assuming you have not implemented any of the strategies I've mentioned in the chapter on securing your stored data, you may want to implement a suite solution rather than the individual ones. If however you have implemented some of the individual solutions and you merely need to supplement with some additional ones then using the strategies previously mentioned will work for you. If you prefer to go for an all in one suite solution, then a solution like the Lightpoint Security suite would work for you. The company was founded by former employees of the National Security Agency (NSA), so you can be pretty confident that they know their stuff.

Another software suite that offers similar tools for SME's is Infrascale. Their products are designed to protect all of your company's devices including protecting you from ransomware and providing disaster recovery solutions.

## CHAPTER 23

# Is Your Business Being Held To Ransom?

In the chapter on ransomware in the previous section I talked about what ransomware was and how individuals can protect themselves against it. Much of the advice in that chapter also applies to SME's. For this chapter I'm including more business specific information than previously.

## Protection from ransomware

It seems no matter where you look, there are reports of yet another company's data being locked and held to ransom by shadowy hackers. In a lot of cases, the data doesn't get unlocked even after the ransom has been paid. These attacks now number in the hundreds of thousands a year, and generate tens of millions of dollars for the perpetrators from unprepared businesses. You can help mitigate these attacks by using services that let you configure your firewall to neutralise ransomware. Another option is to have secure backups that are stored separately to your live data.

As mentioned previously, the most extensive ransomware attack to date was the WannaCry ransomware attack. Organisations hit by the attacks, which locked up computer systems until the victims paid a ransom, included Britain's National Health Service, French car manufacturer Renault, and Spain's Telefonica. Companies that were not prepared for WannaCry were expected to rack up business interruption costs that far exceed the ransomware payment.

A ransomware infection often starts with someone clicking on what looks like an innocent attachment, and it can be a headache for companies of all sizes if vital files and documents (think spreadsheets and invoices) are suddenly encrypted and inaccessible. But that's not the only way to get infected.

Cyber-criminals didn't use to be so obvious. If hackers infiltrated your corporate network, they would do everything possible to avoid detection. It was in their best interests not to alert a victim that they'd fallen victim to a cyber-criminal.

But now, if you are attacked with file-encrypting ransomware, criminals will brazenly announce they're holding your corporate data hostage until you pay a ransom in order to get it back. It might sound too simple, but it's working. Cyber-criminals pocketed over $1bn from ransomware attacks during 2016 alone.

## The cost of a ransomware attack

Obviously, the most immediate cost associated with becoming infected with ransomware - if paid - is the ransom demand, which can depend on the type of ransomware or the size of your organisation.

Recent research revealed that a quarter of companies which paid a ransom paid over GBP£5,000 to retrieve their encrypted data, while a further quarter paid hackers between GBP£3,000 and GBP£5,000.

The most common ransom paid amongst small and medium-sized businesses was between GBP£500 and GBP£1500, proving that there's still easy money to be made from targeting organisations of this size.

There are also examples of high-profile targets paying five-figure fees in order to regain access to their encrypted networks and their files, especially in cases where criminals threaten to delete data if they're not paid.

Ultimately, whatever the size of your company, time is money and the longer your network is down because of malware, the more it's going to cost your business.

Even if you regain access to your encrypted documents by paying a ransom, there will be additional costs on top of that. In order to avoid future attacks - especially if you've been marked as an easy target - be prepared to invest in additional cyber security software and to pay for additional staff training.

There's also the risk of customers losing trust in your business because of poor cyber security and taking their custom elsewhere.

## Why are small businesses targets for ransomware?

Small and medium-sized businesses are a popular target because they tend to have poorer cyber security than large organisations. That's where I hope this book can help you to address that. Despite the fact they are an easy target many SMEs falsely believe they're too small to be targeted. If that's what you think, remember this - even a 'smaller' ransom of a few hundred dollars is still highly profitable for cyber-criminals. This is especially true if they have targeted hundreds or even thousands of businesses.

## Bitcoin and ransomware

The rise of cryptocurrencies like Bitcoin has made it easy for cyber-criminals to secretly receive payments extorted with this type of malware, without the risk of the authorities being able to identify the perpetrators. The secure, untraceable method of making payments - victims are asked to make a payment to a bitcoin address - makes it the perfect currency for criminals who want their financial activities to remain hidden.

## Preventing a ransomware attack

With email being by far the most popular attack vector for ransomware, you should provide employees with training on how to spot an incoming malware attack. Even picking up on little indicators like poor formatting or that an email purporting to be from 'Microsoft Security' is sent from an obscure address which doesn't even contain the word Microsoft within it might save your network from infection. The same security policies that protect you from malware attacks in general will go some way towards protecting your company from ransom demands too.

There's also something to be said for enabling employees to learn from making mistakes while within a safe environment. For example, one firm has developed an interactive video experience which allows its employees to make decisions on a series of events then find out the consequences of those at the end. This enables them to learn from their mistakes without suffering any of the actual consequences.

On a technical level, stopping employees from being able to enable macros is a big step towards ensuring that they can't unwittingly run a ransomware file. Microsoft Office 2016 - and now Microsoft 2013 - both carry features which allow macros to be disabled. At the very least, as a business you should invest in anti-virus software and keep it up-to date, so that it can warn users about potentially malicious files. Backing up important files and making sure those files can't be compromised during an attack in another key.

## Getting rid of ransomware

The 'No More Ransom' initiative launched in July 2016 by Europol and the Dutch National Police in collaboration with a number of cyber security companies offers free decryption tools for ransomware variants to help victims retrieve their encrypted data without succumbing to the will of cyber extortionists. You can find more information on this in the earlier chapter on ransomware for individuals.

Another way of working around a ransomware infection is to ensure your organisation regularly backs up data offline. It might take some time to transfer the backup files onto a new machine, but if a computer is infected and you have backups, it's possible just to isolate that unit then get on with your business. Just make sure that crypto-locking crooks aren't able to encrypt your back-ups too.

## CHAPTER 24

# Ensure You're Insured

When bad stuff does happen, and all your defences have failed, it's a good idea to have something in place to offset the potentially huge costs of a cyber failure in your business. Yes, I'm talking about insurance.

Nearly nine out 10 cyber insurance policies in the world are in the United States, according to Kevin Kalinich, global head of Aon Plc's cyber risk practice. The annual premium market stands at $2.5-$3 billion.

Probably the biggest single reason for the larger penetration in the United States is that U.S. businesses have had to comply with state breach notification laws for the past 10 years.

That greater transparency created an incentive for U.S. companies to get insurance to compensate for damage from incidents they were required to report. Many companies outside the United States may not have cover for computer-system attacks (leaving them potentially with millions of dollars of losses to bear), because there has been relatively little take-up of cyber insurance, according to insurers. That situation is expected to change however, since even before the attacks, demand in Europe was expected to rise after an EU directive is implemented in mid-2018 requiring companies to notify authorities of a data breach.

A typical cyber insurance policy will protect companies against extortion like ransomware attacks, which insurers say have spiked recently. It should cover the investigation costs and also pay the ransom. Cyber insurance policies also typically cover the cost of notifying those whose data has been breached, hiring a PR agency to address reputational damage, and arranging credit monitoring for those affected, as well as potential legal suits.

Most cyber insurance policies cover breaches of up to $50 million, with much of the losses related to the interruption of the firms' business. Some policies can cover losses for as much as $500-600 million.

It is a high-margin business for the insurance companies though. Insurer Sciemus, for example, has previously said it charges around $100,000 for $10 million in data breach insurance and as much as seven times that to cover attacks causing physical damage.

Other providers include Allianz, AIG, Chubb and Zurich as well as Lloyds' of London insurers such as Beazley and Hiscox.

But there are caveats to this. It is insurance after all, and aren't there always loopholes? In the WannaCry attack for example, companies that did not download a Microsoft patch issued to protect users from vulnerabilities may be out of luck, since many cyber policies exclude coverage in such an instance. Companies using pirated software are also unlikely to be eligible for an insurance pay out. These are really important details to check in your company. You could end up losing a couple of million dollars otherwise, if one of your customers were to sue for example. Also once you have insurance, check the pay out terms. For example, insurers may seek to deny coverage if companies pay the ransom without contacting their insurers first.

It's up to you whether you think there is a good cost benefit argument for insurance in your business, but at least now you know that it exists and what it can do for you.

# CyberSafe Checklist For SME's

The checklist below summarises the content from the SME section and shows you where to find it. You don't need to action on all of it, but clearly the more you complete, the more secure your business will be.

| Action | Chapter Ref | Done |
|---|---|---|
| Get an HTTPS certificate for your website | 21 | |
| Educate your employees on cyber security threats | 17 | |

| Action | Chapter Ref | Done |
|---|---|---|
| Implement access management on your technology infrastructure | 17 | |
| Enforce 2FA on your systems | 17 | |
| Encrypt your hard drives | 19 | |
| Provide VPN's for your mobile workers | 20 | |
| Update all your | 3 | |

| Action | Chapter Ref | Done |
|---|---|---|
| devices with the latest software patches | | |
| Implement DDoS mitigation strategies | 22 | |
| Securely back up your data in the cloud | 23 | |
| Securely back up your data locally | 23 | |
| Pay for cyber insurance | 25 | |

# The Last Word

Almost everything in this book —even changing over your email—can be done in a day, tops. It's just a matter of taking it step by step. If you feel you don't have the technical skills or the time to do it, hire someone you trust to do it for you. If you don't know anyone with the skillset, consider one of the local independent computer shops, and help support your local community.

I hope this book has sufficiently informed you of your options for keeping the sharks of the internet at bay, and ensure that you continue to enjoy a stress free online life. Remember you can use all or none of these strategies depending on your needs. Will all the strategies I've outlined render you completely invulnerable to cyber-attacks? No, but they will make you a damned sight more secure than you were before you opened this book.

As I noted earlier, I haven't mentioned every tool that you can use, but you can find a list of recommended internet tools here at the link below: http://www.expatpat.com/tools. The list is updated on a fairly regular basis.

If you enjoyed the book, and want to be kept updated on evolving cyber threats and how to deal with them, sign up to the CyberSafe alert email newsletter by going to: www.expatpat.com/cybersafealert

# Further Reading

Brazil blocks WhatsApp -
https://techcrunch.com/2016/07/19/whatsapp-
blocked-in-brazil-again/

U.S Government IoT security competition -
https://www.ftc.gov/iot-home-inspector-
challenge

FBI PSA on ransomware -
https://www.ic3.gov/media/2016/160915.aspx

The Code Book - Simon Singh

Kids dolls hacked -
http://www.bbc.com/news/world-europe-
39002142

Edward Snowden and Bunnie Huang built a
privacy add-on for the iPhone -
https://www.fastcompany.com/40466986/edwa
rd-snowden-bunnie-huang-built-a-privacy-
surveillance-add-on-case-for-smartphones-
iphone

Fast Facts About Cyber Security in 2017 - https://investingnews.com/daily/tech-investing/cyber security-investing/infographic-fast-facts-cyber security-2017/

The godfather of ransomware returns - http://www.zdnet.com/article/the-godfather-of-ransomware-returns-locky-is-back-and-sneakier-than-ever/

Republicans Are About To Sell Your Browser History. Here's How To Protect Yourself - http://www.huffingtonpost.com/entry/internet-privacy-protect-yourself_us_58dbe492e4b01ca7b4291bf5?fq7

# Additional Resources

Action Fraud - **The UK's national fraud and cyber-crime reporting centre**

Anti-Phishing Working Group

Asia Policy Partners

Electronic Crimes Task Forces and Working Groups

OnGuardOnline.gov

Onlinethreatalerts.com

Online Trust Alliance

Scam Survivors

Staysafeonline.org

StopFraud.Gov Victims of Fraud Resources

Stop Think Connect - **(Department of Homeland Security)**

U.S. Computer Emergency Readiness Team

# U.S. Department of Justice Cyber-crime Team

# Tools And References

## Chapter 1 - The Threats

Online Identity Risk Calculator

## Chapter 3 - Easy Fixes

Zone Alarm

Little Snitch

Mac Keeper

1Password

Koala Safe

LastPass

Prey

KidRex

Google Junior

## Chapter 4 - Secure Your Stored Data

AES Crypt

AxCrypt

BestCrypt

Challenger

CryptSetup

DiskCryptor

Windows Bitlocker

Mega

Tresorit

Boxcryptor

Spideroak

# Chapter 6 - Internet Browsing

Mozilla Firefox

Tor Browser Bundle

HTTPS Everywhere

Web of Trust (WOT)

CallingID

Let's Encrypt

portableapps.com

freesmug.org

Orbot

Orweb

Onion BrowserTorproject.org

i2p2.de

Cryptohippie

Hotspot Shield

Anonymizer

**Chapter 7 - Secure Searching**

DuckDuckGo

Disconnect Me

DoNotTrackMe

NoScript

**Chapter 8 - Email**

SwissMail.org

Neomailbox.net

Secure.runbox.com

Thunderbird

Tutanota

FastMail

Vanish

mailinator

**ThrowAwayMail**

NeoMailBox

Silent Circle.

Pretty Good Privacy (PGP)

Gnu Privacy Guard (GPG)

Open Key Chain

K-9 Mail

Guardian Project

iPGMail

Protonmail

snopes

## Chapter 9 - Secure Chat and Text

TextSecure

Cryptocat

Pidgin

Adium

ChatSecure

## Chapter 10 - Secure Voice Calls

Skype

Google Voice

Whatsapp

Jitsi

Diamondcard.us

CSipSimple

RedPhone

Groundwire app

Silent Phone

Wire

## Chapter 11 - Secure Payments

bitcoin.org

Warp Wallet

Bit Address

## Chapter 12 - Internet of Things

Box

## Chapter 13 - Are You Being Held to Ransom?

No More Ransom (NMR)

## Chapter 14 - SME Introduction

WhiteOps

## Chapter 15 - You Are the Weakest Link

Workplace Security Risk Calculator

Small Business Internet Security Planner

Dolphin by Boonex

Bitrix24

exo Platform

Prey

Computrace

https://www.gov.uk/government/collections/cyber-security-training-for-business

https://www.futurelearn.com/courses/cyber-security-business

## Chapter 16 - Secure Your Gates

http://www.expatpat.com/tools

One login

ID Key1 Password

Encryptr


## Chapter 17 - Go Phish

inky


## Chapter 18 - Get Encrypted

paubox


## Chapter 19 - Trading Your IP for a Sandwich

Dispel


## Chapter 20 - Safe Commerce

Let's Encrypt

escrow.com

payoneer

## Chapter 21 - Don't Be Denied Service

Akamai

CloudFlare

Incapsula

AWS Shield

Denominator

Namebench

Bromium

website risk grader

Spoofer

## Chapter 22 -  Let's Backup a Bit

Lightpoint Security

Infrascale


## Chapter 24 -  Ensure You're Insured

Beazley

Hiscox

# Glossary

## ActiveX

ActiveX is a loosely defined set of technologies developed by Microsoft in 1996 for sharing information among different applications. ActiveX is an outgrowth of two other Microsoft technologies called OLE (Object Linking and Embedding) and COM (Component Object Model). As a moniker, ActiveX can be very confusing because it applies to a whole set of COM-based technologies. Most people, however, think only of ActiveX controls, which represent a specific way of implementing ActiveX technologies. Many Microsoft

Windows applications use ActiveX
controls.

**Index**

**Chapter 21 - Don't Be Denied Service**

245

# AES 128-bit encryption

Short for Advanced Encryption Standard, a symmetric 128-bit block data encryption technique developed by Belgian cryptographers Joan Daemen and Vincent Rijmen. The U.S government adopted the algorithm as its encryption technique in October 2000, replacing the DES encryption it used.

**Related Glossary Terms**

AES-256, Off-the-Record (OTR) cryptographic protocol

**Index**

Chapter 4 - Secure Your Stored Data

# AES-256

Short for Advanced Encryption Standard, a symmetric 256-bit block data encryption technique developed by Belgian cryptographers Joan Daemen and Vincent Rijmen. The U.S government adopted the algorithm as its encryption technique in October 2000, replacing the DES encryption it used.

**Related Glossary Terms**

AES 128-bit encryption

**Index**

**Chapter 4 - Secure Your Stored Data**

# Bitcoin

A digital currency. It is easy to keep offline identities private when using BitCoin. The value of the currency fluctuates considerably, making it difficult to meet a ransom payment exactly.

**Index**
**Chapter 11 - Secure Payments**

# Botnets

A botnet is a group of computers that are controlled from a single source and run related software programs and scripts. While botnets can be used for distributed computing purposes, such as a scientific processing, the term usually refers to multiple computers that have been infected with malicious software.

**Index**
Introduction - Introduction

# Ciphers

In cryptography, cipher text is data that has been encrypted. Cipher text is unreadable until it has been converted into plain text (decrypted) with a key.

**Index**
Chapter 4 - Secure Your Stored Data

# Clickjacking

Clickjacking, or clickjack attack, is a vulnerability used by an attacker to collect an infected user's clicks. The attacker can force the user to do all sort of things from adjusting the user's computer settings to unwittingly sending the user to Web sites that might have malicious code. Also, by taking advantage of Adobe Flash or JavaScript, an attacker could even place a button under or over a legitimate button, making it difficult for users to detect.

**Index**
**Chapter 7 - Secure Searching**

# Crimeware

A type of malicious software that is designed to commit crimes on the Internet. Crimeware may be a virus, spyware or other deceptive piece of software that can be used to commit identity theft and fraud. See also malware.

**Related Glossary Terms**
Malware
**Index**
Chapter 21 - Don't Be Denied Service

# Cross- zone DNS rebinding

DNS rebinding is a form of computer attack. In this attack, a malicious web page causes visitors to run a client-side script that attacks machines elsewhere on the network. In theory, the same-origin policy prevents this from happening: client-side scripts are only allowed to access content on the same host that served the script. Comparing domain names is an essential part of enforcing this policy, so DNS rebinding circumvents this protection by abusing the Domain Name System (DNS).

This attack can be used to breach a private network by causing the victim's web browser to access machines at private IP addresses and return the results to the attacker. It can also be employed to use the victim machine for spamming, distributed denial-of-service attacks or other malicious activities.

**Index**

Chapter 7 - Secure Searching

# Cross-site scripting attacks (XSS

Cross-site scripting (XSS) is a security breach that takes advantage of dynamically generated Web pages. In an XSS attack, a Web application is sent with a script that activates when it is read by an unsuspecting user's browser or by an application that has not protected itself against cross-site scripting. Because dynamic Web sites rely on user input, a malicious user can input malicious script into the page by hiding it within legitimate requests.

**Index**
**Chapter 7 - Secure Searching**

# CSRF attacks

Cross-site request forgery, also known as one-click attack or session riding and abbreviated as CSRF (sometimes pronounced sea-surf[1]) or XSRF, is a type of malicious exploit of a website where unauthorized commands are transmitted from a user that the web application trusts.[2] Unlike cross-site scripting (XSS), which exploits the trust a user has for a particular site, CSRF exploits the trust that a site has in a user's browser.

**Index**
**Chapter 7 - Secure Searching**

# Distributed Denial of Service (DDoS

DDoS is short for Distributed Denial of Service. DDoS is a type of DOS attack where multiple compromised systems, which are often infected with a Trojan, are used to target a single system causing a Denial of Service (DoS) attack. Victims of a DDoS attack consist of both the end targeted system and all systems maliciously used and controlled by the hacker in the distributed attack.

**Index**
**Chapter 21 - Don't Be Denied Service**

# Drive-by downloads

A drive-by download refers to potentially harmful software code that is installed on a person's computer without the user needing to first accept or even be made aware of the software installation.

Drive-by downloads are a form of malware typically found on compromised web pages. By simply "driving by," or visiting the web page, the drive-by download begins to download and is then installed in the background on the computer or mobile device without alerting the user.

**Related Glossary Terms**
Trojans
**Index**
**Chapter 21 - Don't Be Denied Service**

# Electronic Frontier Foundation

The Electronic Frontier Foundation (EFF) is an international non-profit digital rights group based in San Francisco, California. The foundation was formed in July, 1990 by John Gilmore, John Perry Barlow and Mitch Kapor to promote Internet civil liberties.

EFF provides funds for legal defense in court, presents amicus curiae briefs, defends individuals and new technologies from what it considers abusive legal threats, works to expose government malfeasance, provides guidance to the government and courts, organizes political action and mass mailings, supports some new technologies which it believes preserve personal freedoms and online civil liberties, maintains a database and web sites of related news and information, monitors and challenges potential legislation that it believes would infringe on personal liberties and fair use, and solicits a list of what it considers abusive patents with intentions to defeat those that it considers without merit.

**Index**
<u>Chapter 6 - Internet Browsing</u>

# Exe files

In DOS and Windows systems, an EXE file is an executable file with an .EXE extension.

**Index**

**Chapter 17 - Go phish**

# Firewalls

A firewall is a security system designed to prevent unauthorized access on a private network. Firewalls can be implemented as hardware or software.

**Index**
**Chapter 3 - Easy Fixes**

# Java

A high-level programming language that is a commonly used foundation for developing and delivering content on the Web.

**Index**

**Chapter 7 - Secure Searching**

## JavaScript

A scripting language developed by Netscape to enable Web authors to design interactive sites.

**Index**
Chapter 7 - Secure Searching

# Kaspersky

Kaspersky Lab is a Russian multinational cyber security and anti-virus provider headquartered in Moscow, Russia and operated by a holding company in the United Kingdom. It was founded in 1997 by Eugene Kaspersky, who is currently the CEO. Kaspersky Lab develops and sells antivirus, internet security, password management, endpoint security, and other cyber security products and services.

**Index**
**Chapter 12 - Internet of Things**

# Malware

Short for "malicious software", this is a program written to disrupt computers or the networks between them.

**Related Glossary Terms**
Crimeware
**Index**
Chapter 1 - The Threats

# Micro-virtualisation

Micro-virtualization is a technology developed by desktop security firm Bromium to help ensure secure computing environments. Micro-virtualization utilizes a Xen-based security-focused hypervisor called a microvisor that creates hardware-isolated micro virtual machines (micro-VMs) for each computing task that utilizes data originating from an unknown source.

**Index**
**Chapter 21 - Don't Be Denied Service**

# Multi-factor authentication

Multi-factor authentication is a method of computer access control in which a user is granted access only after successfully presenting several separate pieces of evidence to an authentication mechanism – typically at least two of the following categories: knowledge (something they know), possession (something they have), and inherence (something they are).

**Related Glossary Terms**
Two factor authentication
**Index**
Chapter 3 - Easy Fixes

# Off-the-Record (OTR) cryptographic protocol

Off-the-Record Messaging (OTR) is a cryptographic protocol that provides encryption for instant messaging conversations. OTR uses a combination of AES symmetric-key algorithm with 128 bits key length, the Diffie–Hellman key exchange with 1536 bits group size, and the SHA-1 hash function. In addition to authentication and encryption, OTR provides forward secrecy and malleable encryption.

The primary motivation behind the protocol was providing deniable authentication for the conversation participants while keeping conversations confidential, like a private conversation in real life, or off the record in journalism sourcing.

**Related Glossary Terms**
AES 128-bit encryption
**Index**
Chapter 9 - Secure Chat, and Text

# Open source

Generically, open source refers to a program in which the source code is available to the general public for use and/or modification from its original design free of charge, i.e., open. Open source code is typically created as a collaborative effort in which programmers improve upon the code and share the changes within the community. Open source sprouted in the technological community as a response to proprietary software owned by corporations.

**Index**

Introduction - Introduction

# OpenPGP

OpenPGP is a non-proprietary protocol for encrypting email communication using public key cryptography. It is based on the original PGP (Pretty Good Privacy) software. The OpenPGP protocol defines standard formats for encrypted messages, signatures, and certificates for exchanging public keys.

**Index**
**Chapter 8 - Email**

# Partitions

The division memory or mass storage into isolated sections. In computer systems, you can partition a disk, and each partition will behave like a separate disk drive.

**Index**
**Chapter 4 - Secure Your Stored Data**

# Phishers

Individuals that carry out Phishing attacks

**Related Glossary Terms**

Social engineering

**Index**

Chapter 3 - Easy Fixes

# Pwned

Pwn is a leetspeak slang term derived from the verb own, as meaning to appropriate or to conquer to gain ownership. The term implies domination or humiliation of a rival, used primarily in the Internet-based video game culture to taunt an opponent who has just been soundly defeated (e.g., "You just got pwned!").

**Index**
**Chapter 12 - Internet of Things**

# Ransomware

A program that scrambles a computer's files, demanding payment before they can be opened again.

**Related Glossary Terms**

WannaCrypt

**Index**

Chapter 13 - Are you being held to ransom

# RSA

A public-key encryption technology developed by RSA Data Security, Inc.

**Index**

**Chapter 4 - Secure Your Stored Data**

# Social engineering

The act of obtaining or attempting to obtain otherwise secure data by conning an individual into revealing secure information. Social engineering is successful because its victims innately want to trust other people and are naturally helpful.

**Related Glossary Terms**
Phishers, Trojans
**Index**
Chapter 17 - Go phish

# Spoofing

In the context of network security, a spoofing attack is a situation in which one person or program successfully masquerades as another by falsifying data, thereby gaining an illegitimate advantage.

**Index**
**Chapter 1 - The Threats**

# Spyware

Software that covertly gathers user information through the user's Internet connection without his or her knowledge.

**Index**
**Chapter 21 - Don't Be Denied Service**

# The Internet of Things

The ever-growing network of physical objects that feature Internet connectivity and the communication that occurs between these and Internet-enabled devices and systems.

**Index**

**Chapter 12 - Internet of Things**

# Trojans

Trojan, is any malicious computer program which misleads users of its true intent. The term is derived from the Ancient Greek story of the deceptive wooden horse that led to the fall of the city of Troy.

Trojans are generally spread by some form of social engineering, for example where a user is duped into executing an e-mail attachment disguised to be unsuspicious, (e.g., a routine form to be filled in), or by drive-by download. Although their payload can be anything, many modern forms act as a backdoor, contacting a controller which can then have unauthorised access to the affected computer. Trojans may allow an attacker to access users' personal information such as banking information, passwords, or personal identity (IP address). Ransomware attacks are often carried out using a Trojan.

Unlike computer viruses and worms, Trojans generally do not attempt to inject themselves into other files or otherwise propagate themselves.

**Related Glossary Terms**
Drive-by downloads, Social engineering
**Index**
Introduction - Introduction

# Two factor authentication

Two-factor authentication (also known as 2FA) is a method of confirming a user's claimed identity by utilizing a combination of two different components. Two-factor authentication is a type of multi-factor authentication.

A good example from everyday life is the withdrawing of money from a cash machine; only the correct combination of a bank card (something that the user possesses) and a PIN (personal identification number, something that the user knows) allows the transaction to be carried out.

**Related Glossary Terms**
Multi-factor authentication
**Index**
Chapter 16 - Secure your gates

# UDP traffic

The User Datagram Protocol (UDP) is used by apps to deliver a faster stream of information by doing away with error-checking.

**Index**
**Chapter 21 - Don't Be Denied Service**

# Upstream blackholing

With blackhole routing, all the traffic to the attacked DNS or IP address is sent to a "black hole" (null interface or a non-existent server). To be more efficient and avoid affecting network connectivity, it can be managed by the ISP. Black holes refer to places in the network where incoming or outgoing traffic is silently discarded (or "dropped"), without informing the source that the data did not reach its intended recipient.

**Index**
**Chapter 21 - Don't Be Denied Service**

# Virtual Private Network

A virtual private network (VPN) extends a private network across a public network, and enables users to send and receive data across shared or public networks as if their computing devices were directly connected to the private network. Applications running across the VPN may therefore benefit from the functionality, security, and management of the private network.

VPNs may allow employees to securely access a corporate intranet while located outside the office. They are used to securely connect geographically separated offices of an organization, creating one cohesive network. Individual Internet users may secure their wireless transactions with a VPN, to circumvent geo-restrictions and censorship, or to connect to proxy servers for the purpose of protecting personal identity and location. However, some Internet sites block access to known VPN technology to prevent the circumvention of their geo-restrictions.

**Index**

**Chapter 6 - Internet Browsing**

# Viruses

A type of malware that spreads when people do things like inserting USB sticks with viruses in them, and downloading infected files. These are the reason why we are all warned not to open attachments in unexpected emails.

**Index**
**Introduction - Introduction**

# WannaCrypt

WannaCry is a strain of ransomware worm that emerged on May 12, 2017, and quickly spread to infect over 200,000 systems in more than 150 countries.

**Related Glossary Terms**

Ransomware

**Index**

Chapter 13 - Are you being held to ransom

# Whitelist

In Internet terminology, a generic name for a list of e-mail addresses or IP addresses that are considered to be spam free.

**Index**
**Chapter 7 - Secure Searching**

# Worms

A type of virus that can spread from computer to computer by itself.

**Index**

**Introduction - Introduction**

# Zero Knowledge Standard

In cryptography, a zero-knowledge proof or zero-knowledge protocol is a method by which one party (the prover) can prove to another party (the verifier) that a given statement is true, without conveying any information apart from the fact that the statement is indeed true.

**Related Glossary Terms**

Zero-day attacks

**Index**

Chapter 4 - Secure Your Stored Data

# Zero-day attacks

Zero day or a day zero attack is the term used to describe the threat of an unknown security vulnerability in a computer software or application for which either the patch has not been released or the application developers were unaware of or did not have sufficient time to address.

Since the vulnerability is not known in advance, the exploits often occur without the knowledge of the users. A zero day flaw is considered as an important component when designing an application to be efficient and secure.

**Related Glossary Terms**
Zero Knowledge Standard
**Index**
Chapter 3 - Easy Fixes

# About The Author

Patrick Acheampong is on a mission to help you easily safeguard your digital life without confusing you with jargon. A computer studies graduate from the University of Glamorgan in sunny Wales, Patrick has been working with technology since the interweb was in its infancy. Having worked in roles that involved securing digital information and the risks associated with it in large organisations, Patrick gained an insight into what the consequences of loose data security can be.

By consulting with SME's later on in his working life, Patrick gained an appreciation of the challenges faced by SME's -especially those with limited budgets- in managing their cyber risks. With this in mind and with multiple questions about cyber security from friends, he created this book.

Originally from London, UK, Patrick has lived and worked in various parts of the world.

www.ingramcontent.com/pod-product-compliance
Lightning Source LLC
Chambersburg PA
CBHW071105050326
40690CB00008B/1124